Autarkous Homothety Aer Succor Pervading Egested Dossier Omphaloi

Lunan Foster

Autarkous Homothety Aer Succor Pervading Egested Dossier Omphaloi

First Edition September 2025

Written by Lunan Foster

TABLE OF CONTENT

Contents **Page No.**

LIST OF TABLES

LIST OF FIGURES

LIST OF ABBREVIATIONS

CC	Cluster-Coordinator
CSP	Cloud Service Provider
HCIA	Hierarchical-Cluster IaaS provisioning Architecture
IaaS	Infrastructure-as-a-Service
IIAP	Individual Infrastructure Allocation Configuration
InP	Infrastructure Provider
IoS	Internet of Services
IoT	Internet of Things
QoE	Quality of Experience
QoS	Quality of Service
VC	Virtual Cluster
VCG	Vickrey-Clarke-Groves
VDC	Virtual Data Center
VM	Virtual Machine
VR	Virtual Resource

Chapter1:1.1 Introduction

Over the past two decades, the Internet has evolved to reflect a contemporary view of its capability. The Future Internet can be defined, with the assistance of the Expanding Network Infrastructure Foundation, as the association and cooperation of the Internet of Things (IoT), the Internet of Services (IoS), and the Internet of Content (IoC) (V. Issarny, 2011), with an emphasis on information, services, and things. The Internet has exceeded the significance of many previous networking infrastructures by allowing the creation, contribution, sharing, and integration of information, knowledge, and artifacts. For the longest time, the Internet functioned as the world's biggest service backbone. Additionally, the virtual Internet's most current idea often challenges established Internet access and service delivery paradigms. Clustering and grid computing are two examples of computational paradigms that have developed to aid in the realization of this new vision, although they have encountered many challenges. Indeed, the network manipulations associated with these provisioning paradigms are still in their infancy, and the established "Internet Protocol-based" Internet protocol, as well as the substantial financial investment in Internet infrastructure, make any innovative Internet engineering innovation extremely improbable. To keep up with the exponential growth of current applications, these paradigms' networking architectures need to be updated. As a result, the Internet is undergoing fast evolution and is being charged with serving as the platform of the future. As the Internet's popularity has increased, significant issues have emerged. (Tsiatsis, V., 2010).

The new vision for the future Internet is based on a set of criteria that must be met by every service provider to participate in or follow this transformational vision. Additionally, the Potential Internet requires substantial modifications to network infrastructure and content delivery methods. Cloud networking mixes established networking concepts with more recent innovations such as network Virtualization. These technologies lay the way for cloud computing to become a significant trend in future information system development and for the Internet of Service (IoS) to gain widespread awareness. End-user tastes have shifted as a result of recent fast advances, and they are no longer satisfied with the traditional Internet experience provided by an automated host. Rather than that, the increased availability of services and the introduction of new technology were designed to encourage and attract customers to online gaming and video-sharing applications. Consumer (quality of service) requirements for resourced platforms are high, but it is generally anticipated that cloud technologies will help generate new demand as an IT technology. Cloud computing, which includes infrastructures, applications, software, and business processes, is gaining traction as a significant technology paradigm for sharing information (L. Jie Zhang & Q. Zhou, 2009). These services are categorized as IaaS, PaaS, and SaaS. (Z. Lu, J. Wu, & W. Fu, 2010). IaaS is the most simple and practical of them all. The future Internet of Things will be built on a cloud-based infrastructure. As a result, advancements in IaaS cloud infrastructure may assist users in meeting the needs of the Future Internet by providing new resources and technologies that allow them to more efficiently create and manage software and development platforms (R. Moreno-Vozmediano, 2013).

While cloud storage has realized a variety of financial advantages, it has also learned how readily the Internet lends itself to different business models, allowing it to embrace the technology more completely. Many individuals believe that cloud computing will fundamentally alter the internet's architecture, reshaping the way the industry works as a whole. Cloud computing's prospective capabilities enable on-demand deployment of resources, networks, and infrastructures to meet future Internet requirements. Consumers are drawn to the cloud model due to its inherent capabilities, the ability to quickly scale available resources, and the variety of payment options (cost-effective economy of scale). When contemplating the Potential Internet vision, on the other hand, cloud culture tackles many technical problems associated with encapsulating multiple breakthroughs. To enable cloud services to (1) support cloud IaaS databases, (2) continuously provide scalable and elastic tools, (3) securely collaborate and connect, and (4) resolve future issues related to implementing IaaS databases, designing/maintaining flexible cloud infrastructure, (particularly for delivery) and protection, and (in comparison to operational and business services) (R. Moreno-Vozmediano, 2013). Additionally, while vying for high revenue, different Cloud Service Providers (CSPs) strive to fulfill their customers' Quality of Service (QoS) needs.

Cloud computing's broad use has resulted in a vast variety of cluster networking systems dubbed datacenters (DCs). Several independent and varied facilities are connected through a rack and tree paradigm, arranged in a rack configuration, and connected by cable (M. F. Bari, 2013). DCs are service providers' main source of support and resources. DCs are susceptible to changing demand patterns because of their stringent QoS requirements. Additionally, the size of these DCs is increasing. Without a doubt, some clusters have proven to be very difficult to traverse. Virtualization technologies are essential to the deployment of DCs and aid in resource management. CSP priorities are met via effective DC resource use, which satisfies customer QoS requirements and increases sales. To effectively consider the possible futures of Infrastructure-as-a-Service-clouds, the world must address the challenges facing the Internet and Internet-of-Content; similarly, to do so, the world must recognize the Internet's mission and ensure that Internet-of-Service and Infrastructure as a service solution are implemented, both present and future needs are critical.

The design of cloud IaaS resource management system devices is examined in this dissertation to improve DC service usage and supplied facility performance. The optimum management strategy seeks to increase customer loyalty while maintaining CSP profitability.

Cloud computing, as an internet-based computing model, consists of the fundamental computing resources such as hardware and operating system, as well as the ability to load and configure our own applications. This is equivalent to a hosting network providing actual computing and storage resources for you to run your own operating system. To effectively utilize IaaS, the resource requirement management model, which provides the highest degree of control of the three, is required. Scalability and flexibility are the responsibility of the user, not the suppliers.

The IaaS provider is responsible for the hardware and supervises all operations to ensure the servers run properly. Because IaaS enables the creation, distribution, and operation of an infinite number of bespoke programs, maintaining and debugging all of the software and hardware becomes unfeasible for a cloud service provider staff.

Cloud computing has developed into an Infrastructure-as-a-Service (IaaS) platform that offers processing and storage capacity in addition to network bandwidth. A set of virtual nodes and virtual connections may be used to represent a Virtual Network (VN) with Quality of Service (QoS) characteristics. As a result, a range of new technologies, such as sophisticated information technology/network infrastructures, may be hosted. High-performance analysis and grid computing are used in a variety of fields, including environmental modeling and high-energy physics, as well as high-performance science and machine computing, such as climate modeling and grid computing. (Shamsi, J., 2013). (L. Vecchiola, 2009). Because cloud storage reduces the cost of building contemporary infrastructures, businesses using the most cutting-edge, state-of-the-art technologies (such as facebook, skype, etc) are preparing to migrate their applications to the cloud. Increased pressure on cloud service providers characterizes the IaaS (infrastructure-as-a-service) market (CSPs). In terms of commercial goals, CSPs face a much more uphill battle if they want to expand their operations as well as maintain their existing ground position. To address the issue, CSP's have started to establish centralized storage facilities distributed geographically across the globe (Geo-Data Centers) (R. Tudoran, 2014), (D. Ardagna, 2011), and (C. Papagianni, 2013). (F. Wuhib, 2013). They would be able to expand their resource availability while still taking advantage of reduced power costs in some areas. However, this new design, dubbed Geo-Data Centers, is centralized, which may result in inefficient machine resource use. (A. Ahmed, 2013), (S. Zhang, 2014), (I. Houidi, 2008), (F. Samuel, 2013), (B. Kantarci & H. Mouftah, 2017), and (A. Ahmed, 2013). (S. Q. Zhang, 2012).

The below sections will discuss some of the issues and challenges with the use and allocation of DC resources. These sections covers many aspects of DC network administration and resource usage in the IaaS cloud computing paradigm. After that, the dissertation includes resource allocation issues and challenges. Then, motivation towards the research, problem statement and description, objectives of the research Finally, it details the thesis organization for the rest of the research.

1.2 Resource Management Challenges

Resource management entails allocating both physical resources, such as cloud bandwidth and computing capacity to fulfill all of the service providers' demands about the services they offer

(B. Jennings & R. Stadler, 2014). Resource management is one of the most challenging aspects of providing high-performance cloud storage resources. CSPs have recently faced a host of issues and difficulties in managing their DCs efficiently. Stakeholder conditions exacerbate these numerous complications, as it has been discovered that existing datacenters change frequently and new resources are still being made available, in addition to varying user priorities, and that they frequently relate to specific users who require their own set of services. As a result, institutional and corporate researchers started large-scale research initiatives to solve data center resource delivery and usage problems. The relevant institutions launched major research programs to support data center-level resources. Often, the emphasis is on maintaining an acceptable level of QoS for consumers while also adopting cost-cutting measures in data center administration (B. Jennings & R. Stadler, 2014). A CSP's main role is to fulfill clients' infrastructure needs via the negotiation of service quality agreements (SLAs). Additionally, CSPs may pursue many objectives throughout the year, some of which are closely related to data center resource management (B. Jennings & R. Stadler, 2014).

The term "resource management" refers to the management of cloud computing's compute, storage, and network resources. Cloud network management, like compute and storage management is in its infancy. Cloud network administration enables the appropriate connection and communication with virtual services (VR) (e.g., processing and storage). Virtual machines (VMs) and their interconnections are produced, decommissioned, and moved on a complicated basis; they may also be created, decommissioned, or pre-disposed at any moment. Network access in cloud environments is almost always via an external system, except for those that are natively integrated with a Dynamic-Host-Configuration-Protocol or other similar servers (for tasks such as network address translation and internet protocol configuration, which are performed manually) (X. Wen, 2012). (F. Gomez-Folgar, 2012). The first disadvantage that this dissertation will address is the reliance on external management. This provides cloud administrators and machine n/w operators with a streamlined cloud management experience. Numerous controllers have been employed in management systems to address this issue, but none has yet identified a clear method for overcoming it (T. Benson, 2011). (J. F. Joan, 2013). Hybrid network and cloud infrastructure management have the potential to be a viable solution to this issue. Utilizing key network performance indicators as a management metric in the contemporary day often results in a more effective and agile resource allocation mechanism (J. Araujo Wickboldt, 2009).

A second problem is a difficulty of developing clear and open standards, which goes beyond the conundrum of making things excessively complex and makes communication difficult. Fewer than today's frameworks, today's massively distributed and network-intensive applications are willing to use cloud environments due to the lack of strict requirements for their specifications. Other frameworks were required to interface with the application, to provide a better level of experience to the client. Inappropriate system interaction regulation, on the other hand, lowers the management organization's overall efficiency when there is inadequate common knowledge or an unsynchronized event. Proper simulation, in which the optimum model controls the degree of abstraction and information shared, maybe a solution to this issue on a global scale.

The third difficulty highlighted in contemporary management systems is scalability. Traditionally, monitoring and supervision methods are classified. These methods will not function well in cloud settings, where management objects may number in the millions. Additionally, a centralized method imposes additional restrictions, exacerbating the single-point-of-failure problem. To meet cloud needs, it is essential to use a significant number of novel techniques with broad dispersion characteristics, such as scalability, that enable control and maintenance systems to scale effectively. Additionally, there is a need for a performance assessment method that can account for the variation of various CSPs, allowing for the coexistence of many service providers. This layer must provide the flexibility to synchronize with system management solutions such as federated or community cloud services in hierarchical cloud computing systems. Following the part on resource allocation, research will discuss how it is a complicated and interwoven issue.

1.3 Resource Allocation Challenges

There are viable techniques for determining the optimal location of IT services over a long period; cloud storage is very desired and cost-effective for both individual users and companies, but it is far from ideal. Resource allocation is a critical component of a variety of developing data center management issues (A. Rai, 2012). Due to its worth and effectiveness, capital division harmonizes the management structure's performance. Unresolved fundamental issues during the resource acquisition phase often have a negative impact on resource management. Developing a resource distribution strategy that spans the life of service offers a slew of challenges.

The resource modeling and description challenge is the first issue that has been discovered. When dealing in a dynamic, varied cloud storage environment, such as the cloud, having a resource model for the resources assigned to incoming requests is essential. The choices that consumers have access to in addition to fundamental parameters in cloud-based services, and they may be changed throughout the allocation process. When modeling and representing resources, a suitable level of abstraction that enables the resource allocation process to function properly should be considered. Additionally, increased data availability results in increased complexity of resource use, allowing for increased resource efficiency. This notion is referred to as the granularity of the resource's representation model. Additionally, the definition model would benefit service providers by enabling them to showcase their goods and services in the greatest light possible while also assisting their consumers in making their wants and requirements shine brighter (Q. Duan, 2012). Because cloud storage is intended to use several networking services, this idea will include a wide range of technologies, including Ethernet, wireless, and mobile storage. Additionally, activities such as providing large public cloud services may be difficult when Quality-of-Service characteristics such as those of network resources are involved, since the job may need multiple computations for different variables (Q. Duan, 2012). Effective cloud resource modeling (resource description) enables efficient cloud service management while addressing the flexibility issue. Both management tasks in the cloud environment need completion of this modeling.

The second stumbling factor that has been identified is resource exploration. This method entails finding and localizing the most appropriate cloud resources from all accessible sources to meet incoming client requests. Capital exploration and management is a critical concept for cloud resource exchange to be successful. This is achieved via the deployment of an experimental system that balances user expectations and limitations. On the other hand, resource monitoring is critical for guaranteeing that cloud services remain available to customers upon request regardless of their location. Additionally, these methods must operate well in regulated datacenters without degrading performance. This allows background resource monitoring, which helps in the overall resource allocation process in the cloud. Numerous research has been conducted on the issue, many of which drew on prior paradigms, such as computers and experimentation, to offer themselves more space for development by addressing it. Utilizing an n/w virtualization tool was described as beneficial in deciding the design of another situation in a prior study article (I. Houidi, 2009).

The last challenge involves the collection and optimization of techniques. Before determining agreed-upon and cost-effective candidate choices, it is critical to choose the best resource. The resource procurement strategy's objective is to find a resource capable of meeting all of a customer's needs in a timely way while reducing infrastructure use. On the other hand, choosing a big resource set from a selection of possible resources becomes challenging owing to design aspects; variations in design impacts that affect the result. It goes without saying that, given the dynamic nature of the business and the constant change in the consumer market's requirements, selecting from a set of options is not simple. Market participants are required to adapt resource selection to meet the requirements of specific consumers as well as their own objectives. Different optimization algorithms may be employed by service providers to choose effective services that maximize cloud storage capital usage while adhering to customer SLAs (Q. Duan, 2012).

All of these factors have an impact on the capital allocation process's productivity, the degree of resource utilization, and therefore on management's overall performance. Any CSP must have a systematic approach to resource distribution problems. Such an approach benefits both service providers and consumers by resolving many issues related to efficient infrastructure provisioning, regulated service quality, and client SLA loyalty. The purpose of this study is to demonstrate how a comprehensive management framework may help CSPs in addressing IaaS resource usage issues that satisfy customer QoS requirements.

The purpose of this study is to provide a comprehensive management framework to help CSPs in addressing IaaS resource usage issues that satisfy customer Quality of Service requirements. Before that, there are viable techniques for determining the optimal location of IT services over a long period; cloud storage is very desired and cost-effective for both individual users and companies, but it is far from ideal. Resource allocation is a critical component of a variety of developing data center management issues (A. Rai, 2012). Due to its worth and effectiveness, capital division harmonizes the management structure's performance. Unresolved fundamental issues during the resource acquisition phase often have a negative impact on resource management. Developing a resource distribution strategy that spans the life of service offers a slew of challenges.

1.4 Motivation

Computing assets should be supplied and configured in the cloud technology environment in such a manner that CSPs get the most out of their capital and customers get the most out of their applications for the least money. The term Cloud-Resource-Management will be used throughout this research to refer to all software resource pooling services. For a lengthy period, different cloud providers raised the need for a complicated, changing management role, with current worries about privacy being especially significant. In many current management systems, the primary objective for CSPs is to maximize benefit while maintaining a minimal level of customer satisfaction. Consumers struggle to fulfill their stringent service level agreements (SLAs) while also promising lower-cost performance criteria for their services provided concurrently. The fundamental idea is to assist those CSPs and their consumers by developing strategies that are adaptable to changing operational conditions, management settings, and consumer demand variations. As a consequence, cloud IaaS providers urgently need a resource management system that is efficient and well-designed. This kind of program guarantees that both service providers and consumers are satisfied.

Additionally, contemporary control methods are susceptible to attacks exploiting security vulnerabilities, such as rely on network management (e.g., Dynamic Host Configuration Protocol servers and network address translation) (X. Wen, 2012). (F. Gomez-Folgar, 2012). Additionally, new solutions to this constraint make use of several controllers inside the management system. In the majority of existing implementations, such as Wires and Nova, defining a separate controller for each type of operation presents a common disadvantage (OpenStack). The existence of several network and cloud resource controllers ensures resource separation and enables more effective communication and collaboration between these controllers. This has an impact on both the equipment's efficiency and the management system's effectiveness.

Additionally, contemporary systems have a lack of flexibility in the elegance of requirements, in the sense that they need users to have a certain degree of expertise to work with them. The bureaucratic approach to money management is a significant problem that all current management systems face. When a service provider has a wide coverage area, even if remote management is more effective, centralized management is nevertheless utilized. This implies that data centers that are managed by third parties are unable to expand and adapt to various sizes throughout the world, which may be an issue if these networks are used to maintain a company's infrastructure.

Despite all new systems' attempts at effective management, the resource utilization of the majority of current management systems remains a significant impediment due to computational complexity and solution optimality. A recent study indicates that there is an emphasis on resource sharing efficiency, however, there are several obstacles. These challenges resulted in the diversity and heterogeneity of accessible materials. As a result of the battle for resources and the quest for better methods to acquire and utilize them, as well as for better applications for them, new challenges have emerged. Another aspect that contributes to the controller's resource-intensive degree of participation in the cooperation required to maintain track of many controllers.

The aforementioned inadequacies in current resource usage and management methods illustrate a variety of compelling arguments for this study's foundation. To address these concerns, a layered management system has been developed. This operational approach is distinguished by its use of conceptual modeling in conjunction with integrated management. The suggested design addresses several challenges associated with heterogeneous capital, the multi-tenant service model, and changing customer demand. Additionally, this architecture is capable of coping with the increasing rivalry among cloud computing providers.

This dissertation would enable heterogeneous services, account for dispersed resources, monitor customer commitments to service level agreements, and ensure that QoS requirements are met and resource pools are used effectively. These are the cloud management framework requirements in their most precise form. Additionally, the new system governs the CSP's different management objectives. A collection of resource allocation choices may be defined using the proposed structure to create a system for effectively distributing, managing, and assigning the most effective resource. The design was emphasized to guarantee both the credibility of management components and the flexibility of resource management. Rather than settling on a single method to controlling the resource requirements of cloud data centers, the goal was to generate some fresh concepts. This strategy ensures the most effective resource use at the lowest possible cost while maintaining a high level of customer CSP and reducing consumer aggravation. The organization of the control modules and layers ensures scalability and continuity, as well as the correct operation of the operational technologies.

1.5 Problem Statement and Description

Cloud computing is gaining popularity as a paradigm for providing infrastructure and storage as a service, as well as network capacity. A virtual network is composed of virtual nodes, each of which is associated with or linked to a particular Quality of Service (QoS) categorization, as well as much Virtual Communication (VC) sequences. As a result, it is feasible to develop a variety of software applications that need sophisticated IT and network infrastructures. meters, such as climate simulation and particle physics, were used to simulate a complex system containing a large number of entities in the broadest sense, ranging from microscopic particles to macroscopic planets and galaxies, while consuming less computing power and allowing the program to run even faster than conventional science and machine calculation, which employ extremely complex methods (J. Shamsi, 2013).

Cloud computing enables the migration of an increasing number of apps and platforms to the cloud, enabling major companies like Facebook, nf, and skp to outsource their technological development. It is widely believed that IaaS (infrastructure as a service) will grow at an extremely rapid rate (CSPs). It poses a greater threat to CSPs' ability to expand and maximize long-term profits. Businesses operate their globally dispersed data centers (geographically distributed data centers) to meet consumer market needs (R. Tudoran, 2014); (D. Ardagna, 2011). (C. Papagianni, 2013). (2013) (F. Wuhib). While they increase their overall capacity concurrently by taking advantage of lower resource costs in some regions, they also increase the availability of their resource.

However, as the spread of data center architectures known as Geo-Data Centers has increased, it has become more frequent for superfluous computation to occur (A. Ahmed, 2013), (S. Zhang, 2014), (I. Houidi, 2008), (F. Samuel, 2013), (B. Kantarci & H. Mouftah, 2017), and (A. Ahmed, 2013). (Zhang, Q., 2012).

Computing time is reduced when a significant number of IaaS requests are made simultaneously since this results in a big amount of traffic being sent to a single point along with the network, particularly when any additional request is delivered to the same location. Additionally, some have argued that this makes it more difficult to maintain network controllers in systems with strict quality of service (QoS) requirements and where end-users, for example, in the streaming context, may experience a delay. Typically, centralization at the point of attack is seen as a barrier against denial-of-service assaults.

Additionally, the majority of clustering techniques (I. Houidi, 2008), (F. Samuel, 2013), (B. Kantarci & H. Mouftah, 2017), (M. Alicherry & T. Lakshman, 2012), (I. Houidi, 2011), and (Khaled Metwally, 2018), and (J.W. Charles Reiss, 2011) Two-phase provisioning may be utilized when an organization expands and it is known that it will block more resources and use less computational energy. As a result, our distributed infrastructure-as-a-service (IaaS) platform supports a variety of resource allocation and provisioning methods.

1.6 Objectives

From the discussion, it is been established that the resource allocation or assignment, IaaS provisioning, and cost-optimal solution or optimization is a major concern in cloud computing data centers, it has been noted that to solve the problems discussed in sections above, following objectives are finalized:

- Design of cluster-based framework and Hierarchical-Cluster IaaS provisioning Architecture (HCIA).

- Cluster-distributed resource-allocation approach through the geo-distributed data center and cheapest assignment of resources through bidders.
- Infrastructure-as-a-Service (IaaS) provisioning mathematical model: pricing problem and its optimal solution.

The objectives of thesis include the design of the cluster-based framework, Hierarchical-Cluster IaaS provisioning Architecture (HCIA), and Clustered IaaS-Provisioning-Algorithm, Allocation algorithm: Reporting the auction and organizing an auction algorithm for cloud environment. It includes the development cloud environment for implementation. The comparison of the proposed algorithm with the existing algorithm is one of the objectives of the thesis.

The following are the goals of the analysis work presented:

- Guarantee IaaS QoS, protect customers' SLAs and provide an effective IaaS operation.
- Have a range of workable alternatives to the resource distribution issue that adhere to customers' QoS criteria.
- Manage a wide range of data; cloud resource numerical modeling; unified treatment of all available resources
- Interoperability and general applicability are accomplished by component-based technology that is utilizability and adaptability. These two concepts are united to function well and make for easier and more widespread use of the resource repository that is built into cloud infrastructure as well as centralized administration of network services.
- Some synchronization and connectivity problems that cause additional traffic between various controllers are mitigated. Working models and algorithms are capable of addressing this scalability without compromising performance.

- Increase DC usage; as DC utilization rises, more requests are accepted, removing the resource fragmentation issue.
- Increase CSP profits; the CSP's primary goal is to optimize benefit while being constrained by his clients' QoS requirements. The designed structure takes into account the goals of all participants.

1.7 Thesis Organization

The thesis is divided into the following chapters.

Chapter 1. Introduction: This chapter covers, introduction to the basics of cloud computing and its challenges, motivation towards the work. Further, it describes the problem statement and lists the objectives of this thesis. It also provides an overview of algorithms used in the thesis.

Chapter 2. Literature Review: The whole section conducts a literature analysis of recent cloud computing studies. This overview of the cloud computing platform includes a description and compilation of cloud computing functions, service models, and design models. The technology that enables cloud computing is addressed, with a concentration on virtualization. In addition, an example of data centers and their various topologies are shown. There is a short overview of the job relating to data center resource utilization and optimization. A debate on data center energy use was also held. Finally, a short survey of related commercial and open-source cloud infrastructure platforms was undertaken.

Chapter 3. Design of Cluster-based Framework: Current management frameworks' shortcomings and problems are discussed. The proposed framework's layered design is presented based on these constraints. The suggested device goals are presented first. The main supporting technologies that make up the cloud storage ecosystem are represented, and the design provided is broken down layer by layer. Two examples illustrate how a community of consumers communicates with one or more suppliers while accessing services. Eventually, the Infrastructure as a service provisioning cycle is seen to show how different device modules interact and to explain the architecture's operational steps. This research proposes an implementation of a cluster-based framework for IaaS, which enables customers to expertly hosted intensified performance computing applications and CSPs to use their resources beneficially.

The aim is to implement the necessary performance metrics such that Speedup, Efficiency, Elasticity, and Cloud Productivity such that QoS of Cloud, Service Cost, Availability. And enhance the capabilities of the geodata centers to deliver services to the customers with less time consumption and in a more efficient manner rather than before via previous techniques.

Chapte 4. Cluster-distributed resource-allocation approach through geo-distributed data center: This chapter elaborates the analysis of the suggested algorithm under influence of cloud-based resource assignment and reviews the impacts on the working of the algorithm. A cluster-distributed resource-allocation solution has been suggested. Via a geo-distributed data center, we used the Vickrey-Clarke-Groves (VCG) method to understand intrigue and misrepresentation in a cluster-distributed resource-allocation strategy.

Thesis demonstrate this by a simulation in which many bidders compete for a broad contract. The deal is broken down into several assignments. Any functions must be delegated to a bidder since they are important. Others aren't as essential, and if they're left unassigned, they'll be penalized. The aim is to find the most cost-effective way to delegate assignments to bidders. As a result, there must be no collusion between such bidders when it comes to awarding offers.

Chapter 5. The Pricing Problems and its Optimal Solution by Hierarchical-Cluster IaaS provisioning Architecture (HCIA) Model in comparison with previously held RCG-IaaS Model.: The Pricing problem is an important issue for the customers and service providers. This chapter focuses on managing pricing problems and gives optimal solutions for cloud computing services. In this chapter, we focus on the pricing problems and their optimal solution by which it can give the best results by our Hierarchical-Cluster IaaS provisioning Architecture (HCIA) Model in comparison with the previously held RCG-IaaS Model.

Chapter 6. Implementation of algorithms: This chapter explains the thesis implementation work with the environment used to implement these algorithms.

Chapter 7. Results: This chapter describes the thesis work done with the final results and discusses major findings in comparison with the previous model used.

Chapter 8. Conclusion and Future Scope: This chapter concludes the thesis work and discusses major findings of the thesis and after that, it describes the overall future scope of the work in a different era.

Chapter2: 2.1 Introduction

People rely on the information technology sector to complete their job has grown as computing and storage capacities, as well as the explosive development of smart devices, has increased exponentially. Furthermore, the universal availability of high-speed Internet communication technology has helped in the understanding of this dependency. since the availability of high and sophisticated technologies such as video-on-demand., Internet-Service-Provider's and Service-Provider's cannot market their goods to their consumers in a satisfactory manner. Intensive computation and parallel systems, as well as utility computing paradigms such as universal computing, will promote Quality-of-Experience (QoE) & Quality-of-Service (QoS), thus preserving the user. It has become essential to counter the demand for low cost and rising delivery issues concerning service that has brought on the cloud infrastructure paradigm.

Changing to a cloud storage model has lately been the ideal option for SPs to conserve CAPEX rather than upgrade their IT infrastructures. The thesis discussed in this dissertation draws on and expands such technologies to include a cost-effective approach for automating cloud service provisioning in an adaptive and complex manner. This chapter offers the reader a brief rundown of the evolution of the cloud computing model and the main supporting technologies that enable it. The successful research efforts in the fields of cloud resource utilization and optimization are also addressed in this chapter. Finally, the chapter summarizes current cloud management applications that are identical.

Review literature describes previous studies in the areas of IaaS provisioning, networked clouds, and virtualized data centers in this portion.

2.1.1 IaaS Provisioning

To address the key problems of IaaS provisioning: scalability and enhanced computational difficulty, a range of methods have been suggested. Both affect the solution's consistency. The majority of recommendations (B. Kantarci & H. Mouftah, 2017), (S. Zhang, 2014), (A. Ahmed, 2013), (F. Samuel, 2013), (Q. Zhang, 2012), and (M. Alicherry & T. Lakshman, 2012), (I. Houidi, 2008), have used a two-phase, coherent virtual node provisioning approach that focuses on mapping the virtual nodes and then allocating virtual connections to the virtual networks inbound requests may be retrieved from two locations at the same time. On the other side, the following are the main flaws in this centralized, sequential approach:

- 2-phase network and link provisioning could generate a large amount of blocking and transaction demands that aren't served due to a lack of capacity. CSP benefit will be diminished.
- An approach based on averages does not ensure proper provisioning of IaaS and less than satisfactory QoS is gained by any query in the system.

PolyViNE is a solution suggested by (F. Samuel, 2013) By linking the different Infrastructure Providers, expands the field of views that can be obtained on the value network (InPs). before forwarding unpacking the InPs and passing on their local allocations in the routing table, each InP generated a separate resource allocation policy within its own network. It was done over and over again until the whole request was finished. the report goes on to say that the main limitations of PolyVine are poor scaling, high runtime, response time, and overhead computation. This method offers the opportunity to expand all of these issues to provide an array of possible answers while using a decentralized approach.

To divide IaaS requests through several Infrastructure Providers (InP's), (I. Houidi, 2011) One of the ways to propose an approach to use max-cut-flow & I.L.P. methods will be to centralize them by using an ILP model. Many of the issues will occur as a result of its being non-expansive, because it may present issues with scalability. Because of the great efficiency of AWS, IaaS request splits can be unsuitable for certain modern applications.

Houidi, (2008) provided a multi-agent heuristic structure-dependent approach to organizing search results. Each system was assigned a map from which it gained resources and returned back to when it had finished its execution But, therefore, they used a small-scale test to do the same study and found out about the testability and execution capabilities of their strategy. An additional issue with the large-scale use of the algorithm was caused by the rise in communication overheads, slowing the output of the algorithm down.

2.1.2 Networked Clouds

Networking provides a higher level of reliability and security for networks as they grow in size since it enables new clouds to be created as needed. With cloud computing on a distributed platform being such a hot topic, network experts have concentrated on issues relating to the building of IaaS (infrastructure-as-a-service). Two-phase IaaS (a type of clustering, hybrid use model where two server instances are involved) is used in almost all the plans that are mentioned. For starters, computing resources may be used inefficiently. Additionally, the issue of computational scalability and time can arise.

(B. Kantarci & H. Mouftah, 2017) This proposed an innovative virtual network running over IP on the long-of-the-the-the-mill inter-data-center physical backbone. With the authors' proposed procedure, inter-supported TOUA-based redesign of the inter-Data Center network, users with real-time (meaning the present) commitments can expand their capacity without negatively affecting their virtual use. The suppliers have advised that maintenance costs (OPEX) can be significantly reduced by using data centers and network infrastructure, which reduces electricity use, which maintains strong demand.

Networked Cloud Mapping (C. Papagianni, 2013) described the convergence of the symbiosis of both inside and across storage and networking (NCM). The research group was conducted to expand NCM to link VRs to shared substrates, a virtual resource being known as a custom or, separately specified on, virtual node ability. In effect, they made the best-networked computing management issue a MIP of NCM. It was an algorithmic method which they used to deal with the problem. It does not allow for the scaling-up of their process, and thus is already has limited capabilities. It is not suitable for handling large numbers of queries at the same time without crashing.

2.1.3 Virtualized Data Centers

The idea of virtualized data centers with uniform requirements for provisioning is an effective and has augmented framework that helps organizations provision IaaS requirements with reduced latencies when adhering to the different service levels of QoS standards I took a peek at some of the work that was being undertaken in the area.

Virtual Data Centers (VDCs) were launched by (A. Ahmed, 2013) as a Virtual n/w that uses Virtual-Machine's as its terminals While several ideas were advanced to embed several VDCs in the data centers, the writers chose the Greenhead regional management scheme as a means to accomplish this goal. One part of their plan was to organize the details of their personal data and one part was to find out who had sent the data to someone. the amount and carbon savings are allocated by the request are segmented into Data Center data partitions based on monetary expense, energy use, and carbon footprint Instead of making the virtual devices distributed requests and applying filters to them individually, Greenhead allows all VDC requests to go through a single point of entry. This being the case, the project was revised to reflect real-world facts and figures. Reduce network latency for a selected group of servers (Alicherry & Lakshman, 2012) introduced a hierarchical cloud resource sharing scheme through geo-distributed environments. The two-phase search algorithm uses a subgraph collection to partition the services into several sets of nodes and then iterates for each one server in each set until all have been expanded. I'm referring to the cluster-based provisioning system for IaaS, which can scale up to an unlimited amount without intervention. Instead of dealing with cluster administration, which I find very painful, I want to look at offering the capability of provisioning resources across regions.

2.2 Comparative Study of Research

In this section, we have demonstrated the previous research work and proposed research work comparison on behalf of the cluster-based framework.

Table 2.1: Comparative study of previous work & proposed work

Sr. No	Previous Work	Proposed Work
1	Customers should get their high-performance computing systems hosted securely, and cloud service providers can utilize their services profitably, according to a cloud infrastructure-as-a-service (IaaS) concept proposed. (Khaled Metwally, 2018)	This thesis proposes a cluster-based framework for Infrastructure-as-a-Service (IAAS) which enables customers to effectively hosted intensified performance computing applications and cloud service providers (CSPs) to use their resources beneficially.

2	The approach employs a hierarchical infrastructure for managing geo-data centers that are logically organized into regions. (Khaled Metwally, 2018)	The solution incorporates the cluster-based framework which handles the geographical data centers grouped logically in clusters. This cluster-based framework overcomes the challenges of traditional centralized provisioning approaches.
3	This framework overcomes the following: (Khaled Metwally, 2018) Efficient provisioning of IaaS demand. Scale w.r.t. growing no. of IaaS requests. Efficient use of geo-data center computing resources. Guarantee of the stringent QoS requirements of IaaS requests.	The proposed framework overcomes the following: Efficient on-demand IaaS provisioning. Auto-scaling of an increasing number of IaaS requests. Effectively use of Geographical Datacenter computing resources. Maintain Quality of Service parameter requirements for different IaaS requests.
4	Not Done	Incorporate Vickrey-Clarke-Groves (VGC) mechanism to solve dynamic changes in the outcome and collusion issues.
5	Not Done	The solution generated extended to host cloud applications based on pricing problems and how effectively it will work in a changeable environment with cost optimality.
6	To quantify the performance of the RCG-IaaS model vs Two-phase IaaS heuristic provisioning approaches, they used the following performance metrics: (Khaled Metwally, 2018)	To compare the performance of the distributed IaaS system to that of the regional IaaS provisioning model (RCG-IaaS), I use the following additional output metrics:

	Acceptance Ratio: The ratio of accepted IaaS requests to the total submitted requests at each period B. Datacenter resource utilization: The ratio of the resources used (CPU, memory, storage, and bandwidth) to their total capacity in the data center C. CSP's Net profit: The accumulated profit of each RC in each region. Profits calculated based on the bids collected from the successful requests, less the cost of the network resources and the VM's calculated by the model. (J. Shamsi, 2013)	1. The fundamental performance metric is as follows: • Speedup (Su): Increased performance associated with the use of multiple processing nodes rather than a single node. • Efficiency (E): Amount of optimal output (speedup or utilization) that can be achieved (percent) • Elasticity (El): The relative levels of auto-scaling tools in response to workload variance. 2. Productivity in the Cloud: • Web Quality of Operation (QoS): The level of satisfaction with a cloud service or benchmark checking (percent) • Service Cost (Cost): The cost of a cloud service (Computing, Storage, etc.) ($/hour). • Availability (A): The percentage of time the machine is operational and capable of doing productive work. (%)

2.3 Comparative Study of VCG Mechanism

The main purpose of this section of Comparative study of VCG mechanism is that the issues which arise in previous research work done by others not solved the issues of exaggeration and collusion Therefore, this research initiates a comparative study of these VCG-mechanism, in advance by which, this research solve the issues of exaggeration and collusion. & In the end, this research correlating the different VCG mechanisms.

Table 2.2: Comparative study of VCG mechanism

Sr. No.	Topic	Work Done	Year	Journal/Symposium/Conference
1	Exploring the Vickrey-Clarke-Groves Mechanism for Electricity Markets (Pier Giuseppe Sessa et.al., 2017)	We showed that the mechanism results in an incentive compatible dominant strategy Nash equilibrium. Furthermore, this mechanism is socially efficient.	July, 2017	IFAC Papers Online Conference Paper Archive, ScienceDirect, Elsevier
2	The Swiss Reserve Market: Stochastic Programming in Practice (Farzaneh Abbaspourt-orbati et.al., 2016)	The new market-clearing model minimizes expected procurement costs of reserves, while taking reserve dimensioning criteria and market properties into consideration.	March, 2016	IEEE Transactions on Power Systems (Volume: 31, Issue: 2)
3	The VCG Auction in Theory and Practice	The estimation of click-through rates and how to adjust the auctions for broad match search. We	Dec, 2014	American Economic Review vol. 104, no. 5, May 2014 (pp. 442-45)

	(Hal R. Varian et.al., 2014)	also describe some of the practical issues involved in implementing a VCG auction.		
4	Spectrum Auction Design (Cramton, P., 2013)	The combinatorial clock auction is a simple dynamic auction in which bidders bid on packages of lots. Most importantly, the auction allows alternative technologies that require the spectrum to be organized in different ways to compete in a technology-neutral auction.	Feb, 2013	Springer, *Rev Ind Organ* **42,** 161–190
5	Quadratic Core-Selecting Payment Rules for Combinatorial Auctions (Robert W. Day et.al., 2012)	we compute a unique point in the core that minimizes the sum of squared deviations from a reference point, for example, from the Vickrey-Clarke-Groves payments. Analyzing the Karush-Kuhn-Tucker conditions, we demonstrate that the resulting payments can be decomposed into a series of economically	June, 2012	InformsPubsOnline, Vol. 60, No. 3, https://doi.org/10.1287/opre.1110.1024

		meaningful and equitable penalties.		
6	Vickrey-Clarke-groves mechanism (Optimal shill, 2010)	The VCG Mechanism is an example of a combinatorial auction. In the VCG Mechanism, a bid is a valuation. The VCG mechanism then implements an efficient allocation taking the bids at face value. That is, goods are divided among bidders to maximize the sum of reported valuations.	September 3, 2010	Optimal shill bidding in the VCG mechanism, Itai Sher University of Minnesota
7	Vickrey-Clarke-Groves Mechanisms (Jonathan Levin, 2009)	Two items A and B. Bidder values A at 200, B at 100, the budget of 150. Can't bid true values and be assured of staying within the budget. A "straightforward" bid might be 150 for A, 100 for B, and 150 for the pair. But the mechanism will interpret this as saying that the bidder has zero value for B if it is awarded A. Example of a more general problem: complex	Jonathan Levin, Paul Milgrom's Winter 2009	Economics 285, Market Design

		to bid with a budget in a Vickrey auction.		
8	Sealed-bid (Vickrey) auction (Krishna, V., 2002)	It is a simple example of a mechanism: each agent claims its value for an item to an auctioneer, who allocates the item to the highest bidder for the second-highest price. The Vickrey auction is useful because it is non-manipulable, in that the weakly dominant strategy of each agent is to report its true value, and efficiency, in that the item is allocated to the agent with the highest value.	Krishna, 2002	Krishna, V. (2002). Auction Theory. Academic Press.
9	An incentive mechanism such as the Vickrey-Clarke-Groves (VCG) Mechanism (Jackson, M. O., 2000)	we can also prevent manipulation through the misreporting of preferences. However, in many practical settings, it is hard to bound the problem so that such a central authority is feasible.	Jackson, 2000	Jackson, M. O. (2000). Mechanism theory. In the Encyclopedia of Life Support Systems. EOLSS Publishers.

2.4. Cloud Computing perspective towards research

The Internet's future perspective has been influenced by the evolution of new concepts such as "as-a-service." Cloud computing has gained considerable popularity in academia and enterprise as a consequence of these recent concepts, as it allows users to access apps and Internet resources from any platform and from any venue. A virtualization strategy is often used in cloud storage to enable many consumers to use the same services. This latest concept changes the existing IT paradigms and business conditions significantly. Cloud computing has vowed to do solely focusing on commodity pricing similar to that of goods like oil and gas to maximize their profits. This latest paradigm illustrates the major economic change happening in the current digital technology and service provisioning sectors. More businesses are moving their operations to the cloud these days to take advantage of cost savings and excel in the service provisioning sector.

In terms, cloud computing is a large-scale and distributed cloud system in which customers may use a set of virtual and controlled platforms and data in the cloud as well as well as numerous tools that are available to all at the same time and via the internet (J. Kang & K. Sim, 2011). Cloud infrastructure, despite its infancy, is attempting to solve many of the shortcomings inherent in previous paradigms and offers possible benefits for service provisioning. One particular difference is that distinguishes cloud computing from standard deployments is the ability to get the resources on-on-demand. Often, on-such features provide on-the-demand access, pay-as-only options, and the ability to provide additional resources. More and more and more businesses and more people are using cloud infrastructure as a model that helps to remove the pressure of preparing and sets up in the short term but takes longer and time to construct (Q. Zhang, 2010). The cloud computing model is designed to enable users to rapidly provision computing resources that are hosted in networks, applications, servers, and storage without any service disruption, according to NIST (F. Liu, 2012).

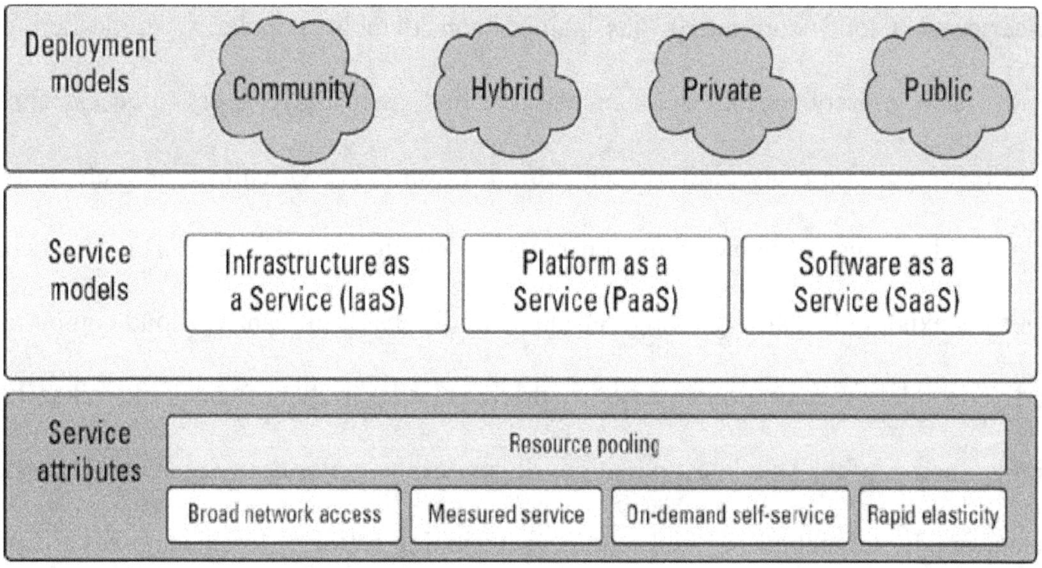

Figure 2.1: Cloud computing's fundamental features, service types, & implementation models (F. Liu, 2012).

The National Institute of Standards and Technology developed a common cloud infrastructure architecture with five fundamental elements, shown in figure 2.1, and three application models, and four configuration models.

Important features include:

- On- self-selective self-service: Customers may request any service and get it installed on demand through a CSP who allows customers to order and receive all of their required services regardless of how complicated the task might be.
- Network interfaces, from Internet Service Provider Service Providers, SMB cloud-based providers, and industry-standard methods provide the service on a broad variety of platforms, with the standard Internet (e.g., palmtops, smartphones, portable mini-laptops).
- An expansion pool that is designed to distribute resources among many customers is an entitlement scheme that is used by a CSP to obtain the resources needed by each. To respond

to an ever-increasing number of customers, this pool of money is made up of both intangible and physical resources that are constantly reallocated in response to demand.

- With Elasticity, resources are dynamically provisioned, posted, based on customer demand, and respond to rapid scalability and variation in ani Elasticity is self-provisioning and self-deploying; resources can be distributed quickly, brought online as well as scaled in line with increases or decreases in demand, and managed remotely
- The type of meter reading, monitoring, metering, and service provided by CSPs provides information and controls and can be used to bill customers, but their application may also be used to ensure and improve utility billing (i.e., only one of which the more you use, the more you pay).

The type of service options offered include:

- SaaS: Users may access software that is stored on the cloud provider's website through this principle. These applications may be used on a variety of smartphones. The network, servers, and operating systems that make up the fundamental infrastructure could be outside the consumer's ability to manage, run, or monitor.
- PaaS: The customer deploys his applications into the cloud platform using the CSP's supported and provided programming languages, databases, and tools. Where the consumer responsibility is focused on specific apps and enabling them, we go beyond hardware and focus on the technology needed for those applications to help customers.
- IaaS: The user also has the option to do common things like storing and running programs, and installing operating systems as well as his/systems, and having the latest features like the latest advancements available. Although the user has no direct authority on the cloud technology, software, operating systems, servers, or enabled computers, he or she may have power over

certain applications, operating system-provisioned ones, setup, and initializing servers, and enabled resources.

Deployment Models

- Private cloud: It is possible to define a private cloud as any cloud that is privately controlled, maintained, and run by a particular organization; whether it is on-premises or off-premises, they are referred to as private clouds.
- Public cloud: allowing customers, companies, and service providers to use cloud storage on a network has no cloud restrictions This infrastructure may be either a for-profit or non-profit but is typically owned and run by a non-profit or for-profit organization. The building which houses the Colorado School of Public Health is near to the building where the center is located.
- Network platform: The common features, such as access and security, are built into a cloud system designed only for a limited number of consumers from a single or a small number of organizations. One or more voluntary organizations might be responsible for its management and operation. As well as using the team's cloud server(s), cloud applications can be stored on-site or off-site.
- Hybrid cloud: Any of the features of this architecture can be traced back to two or three of its predecessors (private, community, or public). A relationship exists between these cloud infrastructures, both of which are formed and patented, that enables data and software to be easily transferred between them.

2.5 Enabling Technologies for Cloud Computing

2.5.1 Virtualization Technology

Virtualization technology is a vital enabler in cloud computing. Virtualization is the method of simulating a user's hardware or software world. The user is presented with either a symbolic association with computing resources or a complete instance of computing resources in the emulated environment. The benefits of this environment over the default setup are various (B. Jennings & R. Stadler, 2014). In an emulated universe, a brand-new virtual asset is created; a brand-new virtual asset, denoted by Virtual-Machine, is made in the simulated reality.

Where many servers are underutilized, virtualization enables storage consolidation, and VMs may be provisioned when desired, saving enterprise money on hardware. Additionally, VMs may be moved seamlessly between physical locations, in contrast to standard computer infrastructure, which is difficult to switch once installed. Virtualization's primary goals are to minimize administration initiative, increase hardware usage, and build a scalable and agile infrastructure. Additionally, virtualized architecture is easy to manage and scale in response to resource demand. Virtualization comes in a variety of flavours, including hardware, applications, laptop, power, bandwidth, and network. The present thesis is interested in hardware virtualization (K. A. Scarfone, 2011).

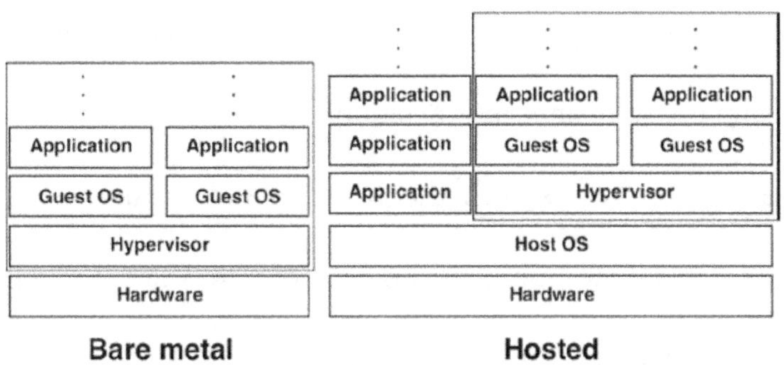

Figure 2.2 Full virtualization architectures (K. A. Scarfone, 2011).

2.5.2 Hypervisor Systems

In cloud storage, the hypervisor is the primary component that allows Server Virtualization. Digital disks are used to achieve data virtualization, whereas Software-Defined-Network

(SDN) technology is used to achieve network virtualization (H. Kim & N. Feamster, 2013). Following that, the underlying foundation of the cloud computing model, NV, is explained. Device virtualization has a Virtual-Machine-Manager (V.M.M.), often known as a hypervisor, and empowers a system to do all the physical one would do, yet more. V.M.M. is in charge of creating and running several virtual machines on a single physical device. Once a real resource is converted to multiple virtual, the sum of the converted resources (as seen in the calculation, the virtualization calculator's output) will be greater than the amount of the original resources (as shown in the calculation, the calculator's output) (Q. Li, 2009). A virtual computer is both software and hardware (its operating system and files are in addition to that of programs and everything else that is described in virtual, and virtual storage) in a modern operating system, virtual memory, and virtual disks, in addition, have to that come to be allocated to it. An additional feature provided by the hypervisor is separation, but not for malicious traffic or data safety, and stability, and it is resource allocation and control for different operating systems. Each VM also has the capability of executing auto-start, auto-restart, and auto-shutdown, making it easier to spin up, stop, and save as required.

The well-recognized hypervisor is Xen the kernel-based virtual machine (K.V.M.) is a complete solution for virtualizing Linux on x86 hardware. K.V.M. is single in the sense that it includes the virtualization architecture into one single package, the whole virtualization module is referred to as KVM.ko. Kernel-VM is a compact, plug-in module-based virtual machine that enables you to operate a guest operating system as a kernel service. Conserving virtual machine physical disk power by extending the logical capacity cuts down on K.M.M. minimizes domain/logical resource contention and reduces the driver-hypervisor relationship because of its exceptional ability to monitor memory and space allocation, the use of K.M.V.

is good for designing cloud storage architectures (Q. Li, 2009). Another common open-source virtual machine manager is Xen, which runs on a single x86-based physical computer hypervisor. For virtualization CPU architectures, like "Xen" offers a feature set that is both reliable and efficient. (D. Chisnall, 2007). Xen supports paravirtualization, which necessitates changes to the operating system for the V.M.M. to interface with it.

Virtualization, in its broadest sense, is the method of constructing a digital version of an object rather than a tangible one. This definition applies to a wide variety of situations. The previously held beliefs about virtualization technologies assumed the devices to be useful in distributed networks and cloud computing was the product of lessons derived from physical systems of design decisions. As part of an effort to isolate various parts of computer hardware for the exclusive use of each or shared use of one process or function, resource virtualization has been created. Virtualization IaaS philosophy, which claims that virtual resources can be completely de-expanded, is at the heart of the virtual resource providers' understanding of the economy.

- Application Virtualization: Provides disconnected access to server networks while concealing the underlying hardware infrastructure knowledge from the end-user to maximize utilization and manageability in cloud computing.
- Disk Virtualization: This strategy pools physical storage units from several networked devices to provide the appearance of a centralized storage structure.
- Network Virtualization (NV): usage of multiplexing (a single path) for the overall isolation of the traffic flow while also revealing the difficulty of the underlying network topology are two techniques that function together to depict the resulting topology.

2.5.3 Virtualization of Networks

In a Network Virtualization Environment (NVE), virtual network administration can make use of forwarding or routing, whether on the network or with other networks that have to be supported by physical networking technology can use their private control protocol; individual service providers or use either forwarding or control mechanisms that are different from the conventional wired link, irrespective of all virtual networks (NMK Choawdhury & R Bouutaba, 2010). Recently, NV has evolved into a core component of the next-generation networking paradigm (NMK Choawdhury & R Bouutaba, 2010). NV has the potential to deal with a wide-ranging requirement while keeping adaptability and low cost. In (J. Carapinha & J. Jimenez, 2009), 4WARD pioneered the popular NV architecture (R. Bless & C. Werle, 2009). The Internet has been remarkably successful in incorporating a wide variety of distributed applications and network technology over the past three decades. However, the Internet's prevalence has been the biggest roadblock to greater growth. The multiple provider aspects of the Internet mean that the addition of new infrastructure or the enhancement of an established infrastructure requires compromise and cooperation between competing stakeholders. The pace of changes to the internet has slowed down significantly, and therefore only basic network optimization options are accessible. Another outcome is that introducing modern infrastructure has become harder than one would expect (T. Anderson, 2005). (J. Turner & D. Taylor, 2005). Virtualization technology, in this context, paves the way for the creation of novel network architectures.

The Internet stopped evolving when it was put in place as a long-term response to the issue of being stuck in one place, preventing users from making changes to content that would remain online indefinitely (J. Turner & D. Taylor, 2005). different VN instances may occur on the same physical infrastructure in NV such that it is possible to connect the pieces without the need for additional software. The Virtual Networking concept divides the overall Network Outlet into subsets, which include self-created social networks; in other words, computer clusters traditional ISPs are distinguished into two groups: the first group consists of the Infrastructure Provider (InP) who is responsible for the infrastructure management and the second of the Service Provider (SP) who places bids for various providers' to request resource allocation in an InPs and then places Bids for various provider pooling and service provisioning through the eNders As a result, a portion of these networks will be designed to take advantage of the abundance of the Internet's inherent characteristics while minimizing or removing inherent weaknesses. Figure 2.3 shows, you can see the major divisions of NV. Expand Virtual Access Point (VAP) separately if VirtualNetworkOperator (VNO) and VirtualNetworkProvider (VNP) are running in separate virtual networks (A. Belbekkouche, 2012).

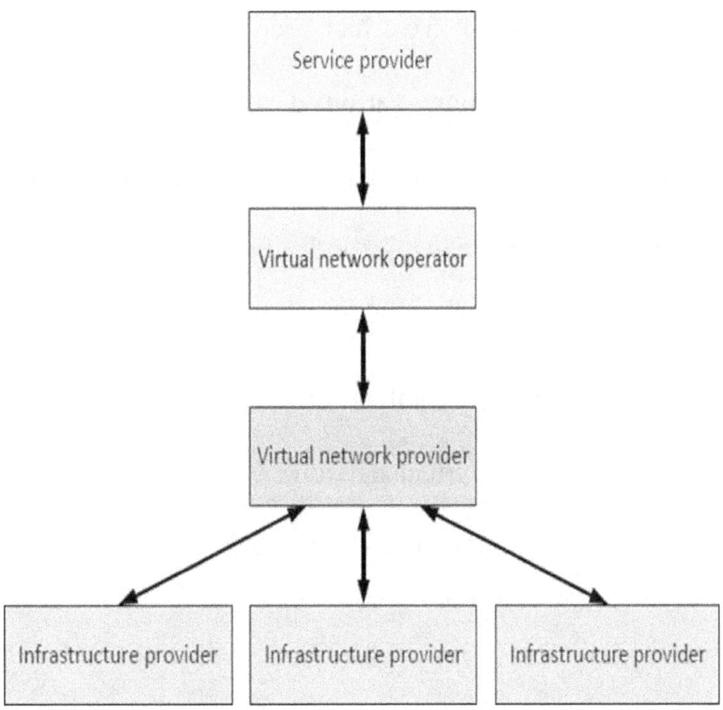

Figure 2.3: N/w-Virtualization for corporate roles (A. Belbekkouche, 2012).

To expand the potential of their Substrate-N/w, they use all available network capacity as expeditiously as possible to accommodate. request from the VNs to simplify and balance the use of SN, the VN embedding method serves as a successful middleman by mapping virtual nodes to substrate nodes/paths. (M. Chowdhury, 2012), (I. Fajjari, 2011). A significant problem for approaches to VN embedding is dynamically provisioning network services between hosted VNs to respond to complex changes in the hosted applications (e.g., (F. Hao, 2010), (J. He, 2008)). Additionally, with today's advancements in cloud computing, NV should be capable of running several homogeneous customizable VNs with varying output objectives. IT organizations have recognized the benefits, importance, and reliability of virtual networks in contrast to the conventional setup. These organizations are considering migration plans to this latest model (J. Carapinha, 2010). Though researchers differ on the importance of VNs, they agree on their advantages over conventional networks' rigidity (N. Chowdhury & R. Boutaba, 2009). the number of attempts to define the perfect virtual network varies. Here are a few qualities that a perfect network have had been reported to have: A valuable virtual network might be characterized by having various desirable features, and by various benefits and by which ones that are reported to be present in its ideal environment: a great virtual may include various advantages, both valuable and of which include being available (N. Chowdhury & R. Boutaba, 2009):

- Inclusiveness: The capacity of SPs to combine different topologies that meet their specific business needs is essential for any virtual network. Networks must be able to handle the problem with any hardware constraint regardless of how small or large the pieces of equipment they are.

- Controllable: Virtual Networks follow a segmented approach that places the physical and network layers on different platforms. We are greatly simplified when it comes to working in a pleasant job setting. If VNs (which I like to think of as Users, a better name for virtual nodes) had all of their basic rights, an ideal Virtual Network will exist.
- Extensible: When looking for such solutions, it must be considered whether or not they can be compact, Scalability would be taken into consideration. Infrastructure Providers (InPs), hardware provides a highly flexible and complex architecture that provides reliable service when servicing many virtual networks without degradations in performance or quality (S. Yeganeh, 2013).
- More independence and stability: It may be achieved by placing functions inside the hardware; for example, many teams must have their code. an island-specific virtual network should be able to maintain its integrity in the face of disruption or resist client dependency, thereby ensuring the security of the individuals or organizations served organizations to maintain reliable functionality, virtual networks should be able to operate when dealing with network problems on their own and return to their previous healthy condition in the event of their failure.
- Support for the latest configurations: When you create a virtual network, be aware of the traditional networking's compatibility with virtualization infrastructure and use standards accordingly. Tracking and maintaining a legacy network is critical for several purposes, including the continuation of a business and its recovery from being taken down.

2.6 Cloud Data Center (DC)

Previously, in standard IT paradigms, SPs ran their programs and stored their data on dedicated clusters of commodity machines and storage. Recently, as the need for high computing capacity grows and new intensive applications are developed, a bottleneck issue has developed. This issue is related to the bandwidth available for inter-node connectivity between cluster nodes. This new issue is incompatible with cloud storage systems, compelling ISPs to seek a solution.

Under the standard networking paradigm, which imposes choke points and expansion points, there is a lot of operational inefficiencies. to maintain pace with the constant growth of cloud technology, data center networks must evolve to service cloud infrastructure providers, as well as cloud datacentres, 's can do complex relocation, the cloud is complicated to use and introduces additional challenges in east-west traffic Datacenter's today are inadequate to handle this amount of data and are unprepared to handle the future increase in data demands. Moreover, this number is on standard datacentre network traffic such as CLOS and Tree traffic patterns should be investigated due to existing traffic percentages indicating that this model should be in the predominant; traffic is more than 75% from east to west and is increasing (D. S. Marcon, 2015). The most cost-effective approach to construct a networking model for large-scale clusters is to interconnect cluster machines utilizing commodity switches and routers, adopting a well-established design known as a data center (DC). The datacentre holds many machines and networking equipment to service a vast range of consumers and plenty of computational power (M. F. Bari, 2013).

CSPs depend heavily on data centers to house their infrastructure and facilities. Famous service companies, such as Google, Facebook, Yahoo, and Amazon, utilize data centers to store and process vast volumes of data and deliver services. The equipment and technology needed to run the larger data centers, such as climate control and electricity need support throughout their operation is very broad.

The Datacenter's networking architecture is made up of the interconnection between the data center and other locations, including WANs, LAN, VPN, and DC LAN were defined by the network infrastructure itself, the network topology, switching facilities, and protocols resulted in the creation of this networking infrastructure (e.g., Ethernet and IP).

The traditional datacentre network topology is depicted in Figure 2.4. The three layers are included in this topology: the core layer, the aggregation layer, and the access layer.

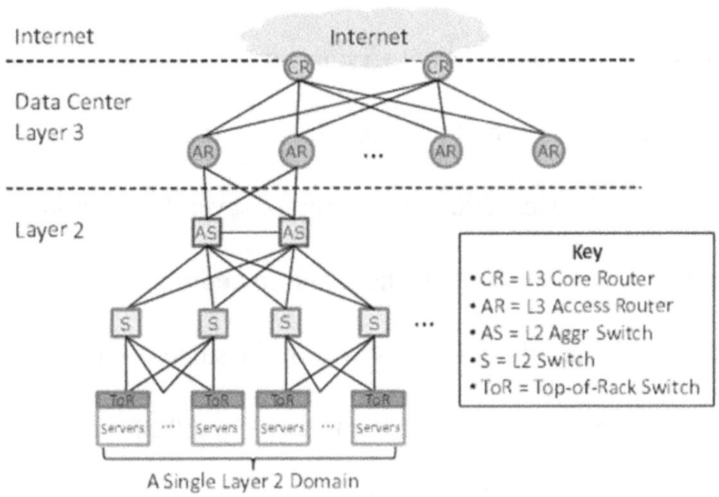

Figure 2.4: Cloud datacentre architecture (A. Greenberg, 2009)

There are a lot of Expand switches in the top rack of each access layer, all of which are connected to the servers in the rack. This extra is a change to the central layer: the switches are being moved from the Agg layer into the ToR aggregation position. ToR DZDs are redundantly attached to one another, or doubly redundant arrangement. These things, which are basically 'local area network switches and main routers, allow the Internet to connect with all the 'at large ISPs and large internet service providers nodes so that they can talk to each other.

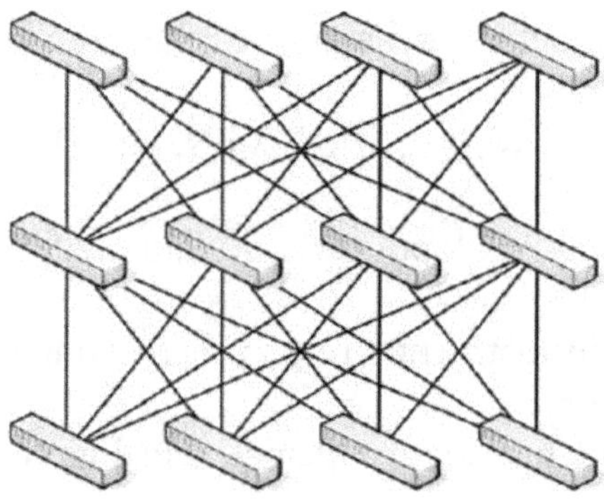

Figure 2.5: Clos topology (M. F. Bari, 2013).

Numerous topologies have been described to characterize the contact between data centers infrastructure. CLOS topology is one of these topologies and is constructed using several layers of switches (W. Dally & B. Towles, 2003). allowing for several route choices is from any level. This approach expands on the previous method, and in addition to connecting each switch to all the other, it also allows them to link every two in the same or one above them. Figure 2.5 shows the 3-stage topologies clos & fat-tree (C. Leiserson, 1985) is a variant of Clos (L-form) network in which data is organized in a tree-like structure as seen in Figure 2.6. The fat-tree topology consists of k-port switches that contain k pods; each pod has two layers: aggregation and hand. k-by-two switches are mounted on each layer. Each layer is outfitted with (k-by-two)2 core switches, each with one pod-attached port. the ninth (or first) port of each "core-Switch" is linked to pod" k-by-two, and each "core switch port in each switch layer is linked to the next in the core layer" pod in two "shelf". Any edge switch connects directly to k-by-two end-hosts; the remaining k-by-two ports on the edge switch are attached to k-by-two assemblage switch ports (M. Al-Fares, 2008).

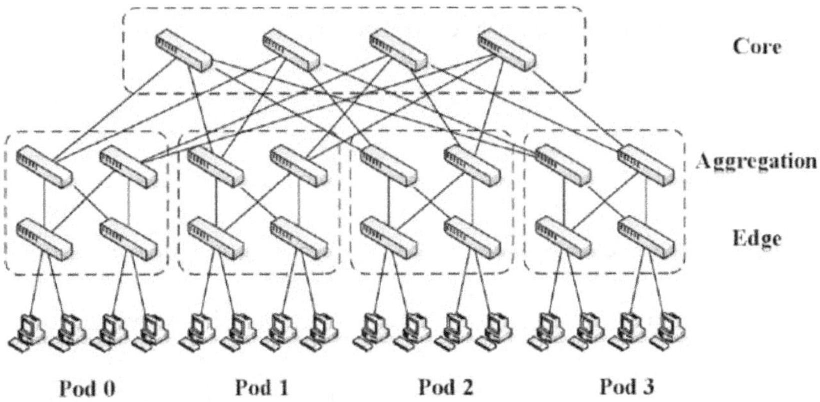

Figure 2.6: K-equal-to-four topology of fat-tree (M. F. Bari, 2013).

cube (C. Guo, 2009), Hypercube, and randomized topologies are becoming more common these days because of the demands for high-capacity datacentres with relatively short turn-around times and faster networks (J.Y. Shin, 2011). We may compare current data center topologies with other recent years by searching for a recent example on the internet (L. Popa, 2010). The primary aim in both cases is to build a flexible topology that does not compromise efficiency; the topology should have a direct influence on network performance and fault tolerance (D. Abts & B. Felderman, 2012).

The datacentre's traffic may be split into two categories: contact moving information (to the north and the west) and moving details (to the east and the west). In the case of remote or internal user-facing networks (e.g., making use of web services), such as in this example, traffic can flow from the user to the application source or the application to the user. Another contrast is of both internal and external connections with the cloud services such as MapReduce, which include machines or nodes that are not part of the cloud. It must be noted that certain tools like searching and parallel processing rely on cooperation, which, in turn, creates additional traffic on the server. Since several businesses are eager to get traditional data center facilities to provide out of order to their clients, much of the traffic goes to the north-south path. Without being affected by the rapid growth of cloud computing, the data center has had to drastically increase its traffic.

2.6.1 Virtualization of data center

Virtualizations effect on data centers is even more extensive since it cuts the actual connections with servers as well as the mutual services that they provide with users. A single physical host may be partitioned into one or more virtual machines (VMs) that share resources using virtualization. Where this won't be enough of a burden on one system yet additional machines are required is supported by the job, this may be a good fit solution. The primary goal of virtualization in this case is the separation and partitioning of the resources of the server. Using server virtualization, database virtualization, and/network virtualization, service virtualization in datacentres allows us to benefit infrastructure security by expanding its availability and reducing network problems such as resource fragmentation.

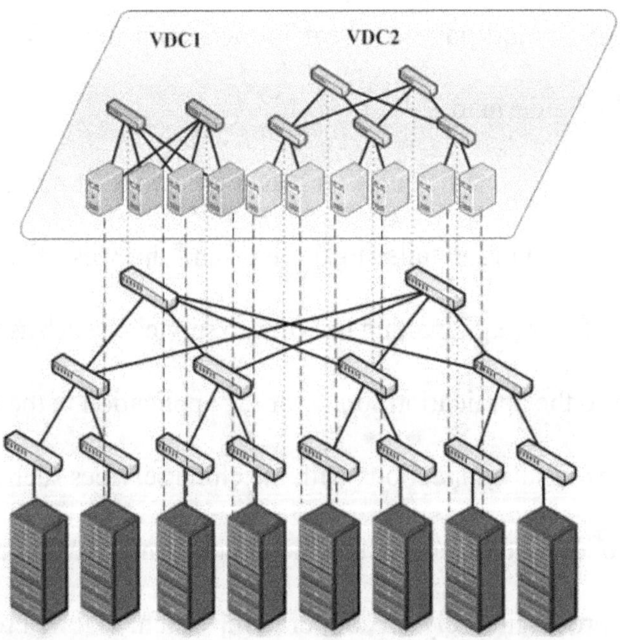

Figure 2.7 Virtualization of a data center (M. F. Bari, 2013).

A software-defined data center (SDDC) that is sometimes going by the name virtual data center, in addition to a virtual data center (VDC) (A. Darabseh, 2015). Network virtualization is a natural addition, thus preparing the network for future implementation of complex, high-level traffic architectures and the use of networking protocols for custom addressing (B. Jennings & R. Stadler, 2014). The emphasis right now is on enabling virtualization technology inside a data centre's network (M. F. Bari, 2013). Since it differentiates networks by QoS policies and segregates traffic for performance separation, In the literature, datacentre network virtualization has received sufficient attention; for example, Second Net (C. Guo, 2010) A virtual data center offers bandwidth that is sufficient for various virtual machines (compute) servers (VDC). In figure 2.7, you will see VDC1 and VDC2 as a kind of virtualized data center with the application of virtualization techniques.

The second Net in example 2 in Figure 2.8 is just one of many agencies responsible for installing VMs on a variable-dedicated cluster depending on the requested bandwidth capacity matrix, as is seen in Figure 2.8. The provision of three distinct types of basic networks fulfils the pledge of Second Net bandwidth: (1) A high-priority end-to-end connection is designated by class 0.

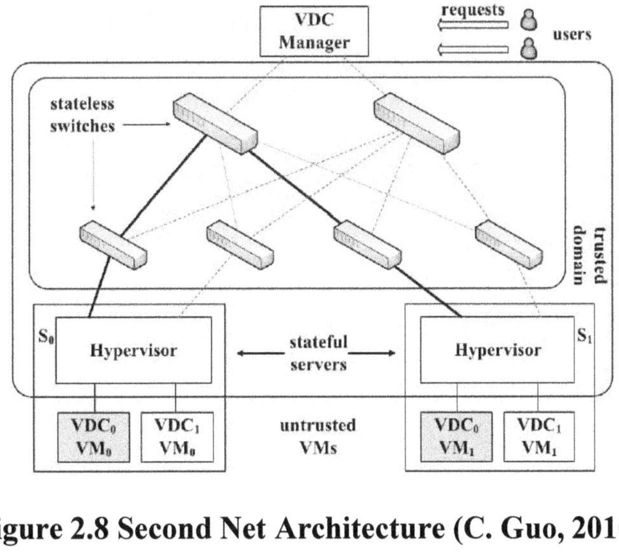

Figure 2.8 Second Net Architecture (C. Guo, 2010).

(2) An important advantage of an award-winning best-service than one where bands are assured to be delivered according to tier 1 and bandwidth with maximum assurance, and (3) a best-effort service is denoted by type 2. The second Net also used a port-switching source routing (PSSR) forwarding mechanism, which is a simplified variant of the MAC address-based forwarding scheme. Port numbers are no longer being used with this new method; rather than names, ports are now being forwarded. However, a network's spatial structure must be well-defined in the case of Second Net, since it refers to a more significant limit. This means that B Cube and fat networks provide efficient network performance; in contrast, V2 and FILL use non-defined networks that degrade their overall quality. The second Net also neglects characteristics essential to efficiency, such as latency.

(H. Rodrigues, 2011) suggested that the idea of "Gatekeeper" be a term to define the difficulty of network performance protection. In multi-tenant data, a bandwidth reservation is given such that you can maximize the amount of bandwidth each VM gets. the authors also believe that a good network output isolation approach should be versatile in regards to the number of virtual machines it runs and predictable in regards to network efficiency Thirdly, the authors provide a solution that is free of tactics, that anybody who wants to can use it, but which is customizable to success around the board. the Gatekeeper examined each pair of VMs to ensure that their transfer bandwidth limits were beyond tolerance. the conclusion is that other applications and current operating systems disregard or ignores latency as a parameter in favor of other functions, features. In addition, Gatekeeper is still in the developmental stages, a full rollout in the real world is needed; moreover, true experiments would have to be done in real-world environments.

Cloud Naas (T. Benson, 2011) This hybrid architecture permits cloud-deploying of business systems, which means deploying and managing virtual applications without relying on dedicated servers. Among the various enabled infrastructure components, application-specific addresses, middlebox traversal is a basic element which is crucial for the functioning of businesses, and reservation of network bandwidth for the exclusive use of selected applications is of course; however, additional primitives involve address groups, VM classification, and reservation of the amount of bandwidth for business use only. The OpenFlow forwarding architecture is adopted by Cloud Naas for forwarding is what is needed by Cloud (e.g., middlebox traversal). Several basic tasks must be accomplished before an application can be deployed in Cloud Naas. These primitives, or foundations, then provide the user with the framework with the parameters necessary to allow for the user to begin function with the required end application definition. These data would allow the application to take the specified application settings and provide the cloud-controller definition. This is followed by the network controller transforming the network parameters into a synchronization matrix. The virtual machine's derived matrix has been used to decide where to position the other VMs, and what transfer configurations to use for each other VMs' traffic expansion. locality currently drives VM placement decisions are weighted in the placement, making the greedy bin-packing heuristic more accurate. Helping Cloud Naas to keep network connectivity and accommodate network policy adjustments by re-updating the VDCs is also nice to have. One downside to Cloud-related congestion due to having just been present on a small route is the use of the network is lowered as a result. More importantly, Cloud Naas also attempts to maintain a good balance between scalability and use.

CSPs offer on-demand networking facilities to consumers by allocating VMs in datacentres, but they make no guarantees about the reliability of the provisioned network infrastructure. The gap between customers' anticipated and actual progress affects the efficiency of datacentre-hosted applications, raising a management issue. Furthermore, inconsistent network performance has a negative influence on application efficiency and, as a result, customer loyalty.

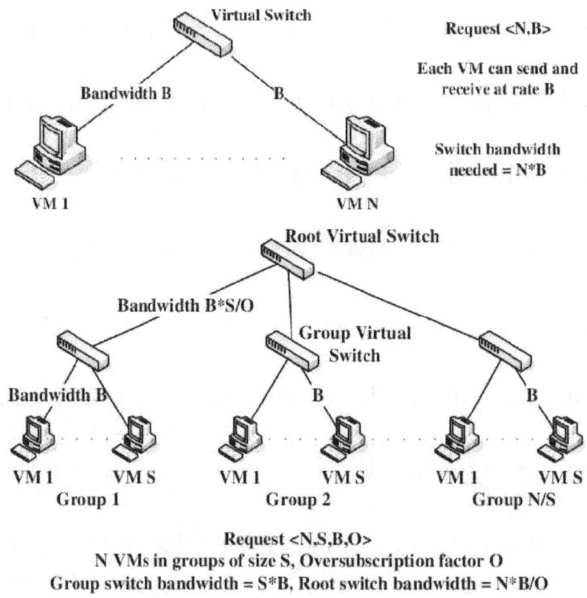

Figure 2.9: Oktopus proposed Abstractions (H. Ballani, 2011).

Both of these causes are related to a drop in revenue. Oktopus (H. Ballani, 2011) has two virtual network abstractions, as seen in Figure 2.9. (A virtual cluster, a higher level of memory use, and an additional measure of memory expansion). This introduction sought to maintain a healthy compromise between the income generated by suppliers and the expense of performance commitments offered to consumers. Not only does Oktopus improve application efficiency, but it also provides greater flexibility for InPs. Additionally, Oktopus enables consumers to strike a compromise between value and expense. These abstractions are relevant to a broad spectrum of cases. A client must choose the requisite abstraction for his or her preferred package, as well as the degree of VN oversubscription, which is determined by the application's communication style (e.g., user-facing web applications, data-intensive applications). Oktopus uses a greedy algorithm to assign control to the VDC and is designed for physical network topologies that mimic trees. The primary drawback of Oktopus is its inability to deal with tree-like network topologies. Thus, the design of Oktopus abstractions for other network topologies remains an open task.

Traditionally, programs have, in the past, seen the problem of the complexity and reliability concerns related to network and system compatibility hidden from customers. Nowadays, though, the software-defined platform is gaining traction to further solve these problems. More or less, the whole datacentre is being handled by computers as opposed to being solely by them is accomplished by the division between the data and control planes, that is, to be controlled entirely by computers is done here. Through fully handling the term has been extended to datacentre technology, what is known about the datacentre's requirements has been discovered and quantified as virtualization, allowing for optimization of it (storage, security, compute, and network). At this stage, the expansion of virtualization and cloud infrastructure, software-defined datacentres are no longer incremental but inevitable. As well as in traditional datacentres, where infrastructure is typically determined by the hardware and the event, there are specialized hardware expansions like this. Through doing this, all datacentre components, particularly networking and the CPU, as well as all other components are decentralized as a service are provided. Regardless of the arguments against it, the software-defined datacentre has three components: network virtualization, server virtualization, and disk virtualization would be adopted widely in the datacentre sector shortly.

2.6.2 Resource Allocation in Cloud data center

Extensively investigated in the literature about datacentre management strategies and allocation procedures are important numerous components have evolved in the majority of these ideas, the allocated resources included positioning and allocation of initial virtual machines (like Linux) was also needed, and fixed-res-output methods (interactive and static) were employed. Research also highlighted the fact that virtual machines (VMs) were typically initiated on physical hosts as opposed to bare metal several years ago. We've seen several designs utilizing a scenario that is close to disk space allocation as a virtual machine distribution in an architecture design dilemma when faced with storage issues where you have many storage resources (parallel array, LUNs, node types, etc.) that need usage models for a single workload. As a result, heuristic algorithms are often proposed and evaluated as promising solutions for problems of this kind, such as (B. Li, 2009), (G. Jung, 2008), (R. Gupta, 2008). Though first-fit-dec. & best-fit dec. search algorithms possess simplicity as the main virtue, the abundance of heuristics offers a burden and opportunity for both using fewer data and implementation.

(X. Meng, 2010) presented a technique for virtual machine placement in which several VMs are consolidated and provisioned to take advantage of predictive multiplexing between different VM workload trends. External constraints are imposed when a collection of VMs is placed. (L. Shi, 2013) looked at several issues such as full deployment, anti-colocation, and stability. (D. Jayasinghe, 2011) using approximation algorithms to overcome three different forms of constraints: placing limits on demand, making things available, and the availability of unknown resources visible.

Once VMs are available throughout the network, customers can perform evolution and architectural structure (or "Refresh and Redistribute") to meet their overall VM configuration and policy changes. In other words, More advantageous than classic (static) database cloning is dynamic expansion, which includes fault detection and simpler server administration. Load-balancing tools such as VMs are supported by the live migration in addition to help a PM scheduler that places of importance that can be made globally scalable and consolidate resources to a smaller pool. For eg, (S. Bazarbayev, 2013), (V. Mann, 2012), (S. Kikuchi & Y. Matsumoto, 2011), (S. Akoush, 2010), (M. R. Hines & K. Gopalan, 2009), (H. Liu, 2009), (M. Nelson, 2005), (C. Clark, 2005) various studies have been conducted to determine the overhead involved with VM live migration, and numerous proposals have been made to simplify the migration (T. Wood, 2007). VMs are started, stopped, fully serialized, and moved to the process manager where they are rescheduled to start over again (C. Clark, 2005).

(U. Sharma, 2011) described a range of approaches for re-scaling, duplicating, duplicate virtual environments, and application deployments on virtual machines Integer Programming (IP) questions are used to formulate these, and cheap greedy (round-rate) solutions are offered as an alternative. expanded on the idea of moving VMs toward CSP, explaining that organizations must adhere to PM service strategy to prevent programs from outgrowing the system capacity while underutilized It also lowers the number of migrations in terms of the virtual machines may increase the overall PM load on the hosts and if they are heavily used, virtual machines must be migrated cautiously. (H. Xu and B. Li, 2011) tried to articulate a modern approach to VM live migration that solves the problem of marital instability called The Stable Marriage Crisis People believe that a “standard” formulation of marriage is preferable to "over-expansion," according to the authors When they compared VM output against migration overhead, they suggested using a polytime algorithm to balance the development of the VMs and PMs at a stable point between those polynomialities.

The great amount of usage of live VM replication and dynamic resource sharing results in the simulation was for the most part responsible for dynamic resource sharing. (N. Bobroff, 2007) presented a method of progressively allocating resources in virtualized worlds, in which case the virtual capital is allocated. As new demands on the system arose, the algorithm automatically moved virtual machines from one host to another, ensuring that corresponding actual needs were fulfilled. an algorithm has cut down on the number of man-hours of maintenance needed for it by accounting for forecasting strategies and calling it a bin-packing heuristic when measuring current demand against historical evidence, developing an estimation of potential demand, and forecasting its change, and altering the VM assignment policy on the fly. as well as an algorithm for placing VMs in cloud was developed by (MHadji & DZeghlache, 2012). As this method was used, it enabled the production team to forecast potential demand patterns, which greatly benefited efficiency and scalability. These patterns were associated with workload fluctuations and addressed the team-related issues that arise due to changes in the flow. the Bin-Packing Numeric Correction of the Mcmf algorithm was previously investigated by the Bin-Packing-Algorithm-developers team, and another rigorous evaluation using an exact Bin-exact formulation was suggested A dynamic model was applied to the above, with a formulation to allow for further variables to be incorporated.

It makes perfect sense to expand VM clusters that interact with one another in the data center topology because the data center network has a tremendous effect on resource allocation. traffic via data center switches (X. Meng, 2010) examined datacenter traffic on a network-aware customer that was contracting with virtual machines with data allowance, while (L. Hu,

2012) focused on network bandwidth management for VMs with parameters that have space allowances tied to them. A variety of other people have proposed to do the same as well, but these methods may have little effect (X. Wen, 2012), (D. Jayasinghe, 2011), (D. Shastava, 2011).

(Q. Zhang, 2012) took an in-depth look at hierarchical VM positioning in the small and large-scale geo-distributed cloud datacenters that were going through their phases of distributed news. Although lowering prices aimed at costs while protecting service levels was a big band was their overall target, the goal of the writers was to lower both hosting costs and capital costs. Operational strategies and game theory were used to expand their areas of control and their areas of competition. it has been studied to determine (and predict) the possibility of clouds being spread out over a wider area in the n/k conscious virtual machine location (M. Alicherry & T. Lakshman, 2012). They recommended algorithms for placement virtual machine coordinates to predict where each data center virtual machine could be located and where to put it inside the data center.

In summary, a study dedicated to accomplishing various purposes, including improving capital use is plentiful and excellent, for example, increased economic performance, which can be applied to a wide variety of situations (O. Biran, 2012). The highest priorities that a data center manager has are the use of their services effectively and uptime, low fault occurrences, and downtime that is round-the-the-clock and error-free. Many difficult optimization problems have an NP-hardness proof associated with them, but this one, in particular, has an NP-hardness expansion. (Coffman, E. G., 1997).

2.6.3 Resource Allocation Optimization Work

Recent study proposals have used a variety of resource allocation optimization strategies inspired by a variety of goals and priorities, such as Context-aware (S. Ghasemi-Falavarjani, 2015), Network-aware (M. Alicherry & T. Lakshman, 2012), SLA-aware (V. Emeakaroha, 2011), and Cost-aware (U. Sharma, 2011), most investors are more interested in businesses that use or plan to use less oil, while a small percentage emphasis on energy awareness does benefit the majority Variety of methods including linear programming, meta-heuristic, computational algorithms, and mathematical approaches have been suggested to enhance the allocation mechanism. This means that achieving the various other management goals will be important to doing so, hence, distribution of resources is imperative. Resource allocation algorithms are introduced in (L. Wu, 2011) to minimize maintenance costs and SLA breaches. In addition, the algorithms consider customer QoS (response time) as well as infrastructure parameters (service activation time). In a further effort to consider SaaS consumer workflow and IaaS assignment, the authors developed an ILP system for SaaS clients (T. Genez, 2012), to protect its consumers from SLA breaches, the organization was created, and to ensure compliance from the third-party IaaS suppliers, the compliance layer was added, Therefore, two heuristic algorithms have been developed for solving the relaxed integer programming and heuristic integer solutions to obtain feasible solutions for ILP has been established.

An algorithm suggests evolutionary algorithms for composite SaaS management/solution of initial positioning and resource optimization issues (Z. Yusoh & M. Tang, 2012). There are efforts to diminish the time taken to operate the SaaS-enabled methods while growing the use of capital. The same authors also suggested a composition technique that consisted of a genetic algorithm and weighting techniques to assemble multiple SaaS components and used a penalty-based methodology to generate additional weighting information (Zeratul Izzah Mohd Yusoh, 2012). They used to complicate the issues of resource usage by looking at them as groups rather than just a list of instances.

Bod (2012) a detailed investigation of large-scale computing in all aspects, which he did for several reasons, including its touch-to-sensor trends. As described in the study, the authors postulated and the potential of a novel optimization strategy. When the observed network topology in the project extends outside the confines of the theoretical expectations, this project was designed to take advantage of the skewness of the propagation to reduce bandwidth use in the heart. On the other hand, the new architecture permits the existence of bandwidth economy of resources thus ensuring that the device is more stable.

the goal of value optimization of the company CSP investigated ways of using Service Level Agreements to increase revenues when allocating its capital according to SLAs (G. Feng, 2012). To determine an optimal distribution of resources according to the requested performance level of service (time, process, and budget), writers developed a mathematical formula for the resource allocation problem which considered the availability of resources, distribution length, and pricing methods. After first breaking customers down into M (Minimum), M (Medium), and M (Maximum), they sought to ensure maximum revenue for each service and then assigned the appropriate number of servers to each. when cloud pricing dynamic pricing incorporates revenues to solve the dilemma of a cloud's dynamic capacity needs, (Hong and Baochun, 2013) suggested a revenue-maximization strategy to resolve the variable-capacity issue (H. Xu & B. Li, 2013). In the planned implementation, the variable reward approach, the income distributional assumption is assumed to be stochastic. Through the examination of the existence of price discrimination and systemic incentives, they also clarified the concept of optimality conditions. In recent years, the paradigm has also been applied to several non-homogeneous requirements outside of homogeneity. The pricing model they used does not consider the many factors that typically go into insurance calculation but estimates how much insurance would cost based on the number of cases and time units of time instead.

2.7 Summary

Review literature describes previous studies in the areas of IaaS provisioning, networked clouds, and virtualized data center. Comparative study of the research on IaaS provisioning of the data center where resources are available on demand and providing consumers with an excellent customer experience is also profitable, CSPs seek to maximize revenues by delivering several different options to satisfy their varied needs. The description of cloud computing perspective in the research and cloud computing enabling technologies have already been discussed briefly in the study on use and optimization in data center. The process of checking cloud resources that have been reviewed on a broad scale has been well executed, Various drawbacks and weaknesses of the new systems were brought to light to highlight their relation to existing issues and pinpoint prospective researches.

Chapter3: 3.1 Introduction

As cloud storage has become more mainstream, vast, and expansive, it has made the need for data centers that can support both simple and complex, as well as expansive. Furthermore, the recent advent of cloud computing as a modern distributed computing architecture has proven desirable because it is cheaper, more reliable, scalable, and better performing than traditional models. However, the fact that the framework has a dynamic characteristic across a variety of markets, such as efficiency computing, social networking, and currently niche markets, including map reduction, has benefited the CSPs in every step of their march toward being influential in the industry. This occurs due to a rise in managed datacenters, an understated technology need, and the increased use of traditional CSPs for centralization, which mostly depend on a single controller collation of data and centralized resource distribution. Fortunately, these techniques are rarely available to certain types of consumers and often require timely and appropriate infrastructure, but do not evolve effectively for many types of services. CSP operating procedures are becoming more complex and take a long time to finish, so the opposite of effective SLA results isn't possible (QoS). As a consequence, scalability issues, system complexity, QoS assurance, and network bandwidth utilization problems are increasing.

In the past, the several datacenters we have demonstrated, the management of IaaS allocation has had a resource allocation issue: We described a sound allocation strategy in a previous segment. The eventual expansion and sub-decomposition of CG through expansion and sub-decomposition of CG ultimately led to a large-scale optimization using the technique of RA (Resource Allocation as a method) CSPs discovered the high scalability and profitability to be beneficial to their business and were, therefore, less concerned about the expense. Data centers show how inefficient the paradigm is when dealing with increased IaaS demands and the coming data center development legislation, however, many major data centers have appeared. Finally, to increase customer satisfaction and mitigate the rapid decrease in affordability of traditional technology, there is a compelling need for a strategy that prioritizes effective infrastructures for cost-effective applications that serve the needs of novel technologies. In this segment, we will use an effective and scalable distributed architecture, where CSPs enable the development of distributed applications and support infrastructures. Each geo-DC is generally requiring its cluster of global data stores, as age-in-dependent models anticipate since age-dependent data centers say. Whereas a hierarchical architecture serves order provides structure, and decentralized systems workflows, the expanded architecture combines two distinct structures in a more integrated fashion. efficient policies and systems under which successful economies both expand and help economies flourish are effective in creating long-term economic structures and profitable organizations can see long-term success Additionally, RCI offerings are supported by the application of a service model (RCAM) at the state (at the state, LC level) which helps with resource segmentation and decentralization. This acts as the basic foundation for two fully autonomous strategies, and it can be phrased as follows: A multivariable optimization model focuses on optimizations on the size of a company, as opposed to single variable ones.

Cloud computing has arisen as a collaborative dispersed computing model in the modern past. Notable instances include immersive applications (for example, the web marketplace 'eBay' and social networking sites) (Wuhib, 2013), resource-intensive applications (for example, data-intensive search engines (J. Shamsi, 2013) and high-performance computing applications (Vecchiola, 2009)), and analytic models built on variants of the MapReduce computational paradigm (Talia, 2013). A popular thought goes, where HPC is involved: It seems as if grid computing is an extension of today's latest activities, high-performance computing, which are primarily concerned with advancing high-scale scientific and grid applications (Mian and Martin, 2012), such as climate modeling and high-energy physics (Tudoran, 2014). Numerous computation-intensive technologies that have arisen and are spread through geographically dispersed locations benefit from this potential for dissemination, for example, high-bandwidth sensor applications that generate streaming data (Irwin, 2010), Additionally, business-critical applications such as weather radar and video surveillance systems, including risk calculations in banking, were developed during this period (Shen, 2015).

CSPs are currently limited by a shortage of funding and an exponential increase in technology needs for hosting modern large-scale applications. Additionally, moving enterprise applications to the cloud, especially mission-critical applications present new difficulties and application-specific constraints (Sripanidkulchai, 2010). Another tough IaaS obstacle for CSP is fast distribution, but at the expense of growing prices, so we should be careful about running a lot of applications, even though they aren't required right away. Most of these problems are multiplied as CSPs choose to have greater long-term financial sustainability as well as they want to extend their geographical scope. So many conflicting hypotheses have explored various elements of these subjects that we are inclined to conclude that this literature is a mess. As numerous technologies have been created to assist CSPs with hosting large-scale web-based applications, numerous ideas have been proposed. Like other technological innovations, cloud infrastructure is a mixture of technology, methodology, and business practice. Virtual computers are central to that because integrating them is at the core of services and networking, and this process is called virtual network embedding. The VNE problem has received a lot of attention in the academic literature, with several problems raised.

Most of the challenges may be attributed to the solutions' scalability and accuracy, or they have to do with computational advances. This means that the issues have to do with scale and the extent of the solution approaches implementable in a fair amount of time.

The researchers at BANAI-Pho expanded their capacity to easily manage the mapping of virtual nodes and connections (i.e., Virtual nodes and connections that were previously unable to map) (I. Houidi, 2008). The authors developed, applied, and validated a distributed mapping algorithm focused on a multi-agent system in which multiple agents coordinated and synchronized the negotiation and synchronization between substrate nodes. However, in their proposal (I. Houidi, 2011), Expand on the order as split using Max-Flow Min-Cut rates for different in various regions, and places it is taken to broader scale based on the total business requirement for papers, using additional Turkerconco, Inc. By utilizing Max-Cut and Mixed Integer Fixed-Step flow software, the VTN request is spread out over many workflows using several rules, each one of which uses both the integer and variable minimum value algorithms (MIP). The tragic part of this is that many of these proposals are predicated on a mixed integer programming (MIP) implementation, which unfortunately exists only in a consolidated manner. a work that is practically getting out of control, as it spans multiple places and involves large amounts of services is challenging to scale. Additionally, breaking VN requests can result in inefficiency and is incompatible with a large number of recent applications. Additionally, scaling agent-based algorithms to thousands of substrate nodes imposes extra coordination overhead on agents.

Samuel (2013) was told that we try PolyVINE, a distributed embedding method The PolyVine distributed framework introduced a protocol for VM embedding and at the same time synchronized the non-SP parts to preserve their pricing integrity. Before adding another router providing expandability, each InP defined and administered its own rules for allocating resources within its network, following these rules. To promote contact among the participating InPs, a global connection has been created. The procedure was repeated before the whole request was embedded. However, PolyViNE dynamically partitioned requests among InPs. Additionally, it operated through a multi-stage distributed embedding, which added to the communication overhead associated with selecting the lowest price at each point. Additionally, the writers discussed critical PolyViNE problems such as scalability, reaction time, and computing overhead.

Current initiatives in the cloud networking sense have discussed resource sharing on virtual networks with varying goals and priorities. These plans used a variety of methods to include non-native alternatives. However, the bulk of study in that area has focused on centralized structures rather than hierarchical architectures. Zhang (2012) proposed a control- and game-theoretic approach for competitive service positioning in a geographically dispersed cloud setting. Their approach continuously optimized the target goal over time in reaction to shifts in demand and resource prices. However, by creating an analysis and prediction module, it was possible to use a control model to conduct dynamic positioning. In this situation, the expected outcome's accuracy greatly affects how good the system, part, or condition is, and this has a very strong impact on optimal positioning and performance. It is furthermore possible to reduce the approach's convergence time by using the game-defined Nash equilibrium. As a result, the system's reaction time and consumer loyalty suffer.

Ahmed (2013) adapted virtual networks (in VNs) with virtual machines (VPs) as end-points and represented VDCs as an end-to-unit virtual network (ENV VN) as they were an earlier use of the expression, Green Head, was employed to describe a method for using the VDCs scattered in the different regions. The authors were effective in getting the findings they wanted since they employed a two-step approach. The first step is to segment VDC requests such that inter-to-partition bandwidth is kept to a minimum, and extra room is made available for all the other requests. Using the original algorithm developed by Louvain (Blondel, 2008), the VDC (i.e., virtual Datacenter) dilemma was cracked. If you've identified which partitions to be set aside, place them in data centers depending on the cost of electricity, the energy sustainability, carbon footprint, and energy supply per unit of each data center, you can now expand the assignment. Ahmed (2013) designed a greedy algorithm to accomplish the embedding. however, it needed a well-designed route in which all new VDC requests were forwarded which necessitated the involvement of a central device to route all of these. This method has a substantial effect on the proposed management framework's scalability. Additionally, the proposed solution accomplished its goals by mandating the partitioning of VDC requests among distributed locations to reduce energy costs. This partitioning scheme might not be appropriate for a significant range of modern applications. Additionally, (Papagianni, 2013) mapped the Networked Cloud Mapping (NCM) issue using a centralized model. Additionally, they developed NCM utilizing a MIP formulation, rendering their approach technically infeasible in light of the massive growth in controlled capital and incoming requests. Also with a comfortable MIP, huge numbers remain computationally intractable.

Chen (2013) This cloud-predictive model called the first-phase cut and second-phase search was proposed, which allows first, cutting costs, and then searching for markets to find additional locations; it also has a decentralized architecture; however, it uses an algorithm that approximates this Since the Cut-and-and-Find algorithm does not have a limitless search distance, it needs a terminating condition to minimize unnecessary iterations. Also limiting the number of iterations affects the precision of the search, and hence on the efficiency of the obtained solution.

Most of the related study shares a centralization of distributed architectures: It is evident that the bulk of this collective research did, in nature exchanged distributed architectures. the single framework could still utilize distributed solutions, but there is an extra level of coordination expense, multi-level structures become more difficult with more than a large number of managed resources on top of it, the apparent concern, the models have issues of getting expandability and computational intractability. If distribution capacity increases in size and capacity, so do the need for scalability and technical sophistication. The key purpose of this chapter is to provide a realistic answer to these problems. The project initially introduces a distributed methodology in designing software applications that operate on distributed networks rather than centralized models. We realized that all the data centers are physically situated across the world and determined that adopting a distributed resource management approach was vital to our overall system. Additionally, we concentrated on the technical difficulty that occurs when a vast number of controlled resources and incoming requests are present, an issue that existing structured methods have been unable to address.

The following portions form the remainder of this portion. Section 3.1 provides an outline of the emerging distributed networking model. Section 3.2 discusses the limitations of current centralized structures. Section 3.3 addresses the proposed cluster-based framework's inputs. Section 3.4 outlines the current cluster-based framework in-depth, including the device design and the framework's critical measures. Section 3.5 addresses hierarchical and distributed methods to decentralized resource distribution, as well as the proposed clustered IaaS provisioning algorithm and proposed Hierarchical-Cluster IaaS provisioning Architecture (HCIA). section 3.6 discusses the simulation setting, as well as the performance criteria Section 3.7 brings the chapter to an end with a summary.

3.2 Centralized Model Challenges

The advent of large-scale data centers in reaction to the explosion of modern applications has provided CSPs with an interesting dilemma. On the one hand, CSPs seek to reduce power consumption to save resources, while IaaS users require resource requirements for their applications to be met as efficiently as possible. Additionally, current resource distribution methods face problems for CSPs. These tasks involve allocating resources optimally for IaaS demands in a fair amount of time, efficiently using handled resources, and ensuring the consistency of provisioned infrastructures. These problems become more acute as IaaS demand rises significantly following strict QoS specifications.

Historically, the majority of resource utilization priorities have been accomplished clustered, often dependent on a single node to perform tasks such as load balancing (Lewis, 2014). Many of the current IaaS provisioning schemes rely heavily on centralized resource distribution processes. These methods all have several drawbacks that jeopardize the effectiveness of every centralized solution juggling (Lewis, 2014). The below are the primary disadvantages of these solutions:

Although the central coordinator determines the optimum resource distribution, the environment stays unchanged. This precludes the machine from reacting to unexpected shifts in the atmosphere or even receiving new demands. All coordination signals must pass through the central location, negating the benefits of resource distribution across the network. This problem impairs scalability and results in a device that is inherently fragile balancing (Lewis,

2014).

The advent of distributed computation enables the clustered method to operate in these distributed architectures (Papagianni, 2013), (Ahmed, 2013). Although localized methods are feasible in certain cases, they introduce many complications for large-scale infrastructures distributed through several geographical realms. Additionally, unified methods are often insufficient for operating at such broad scales. Furthermore, such a centralized paradigm is insufficient and inefficient in situations where dispersed design predominates.

Numerous variables and constraints emerge in a mathematical simulation formulation for large-scale resource allocation problems in centralized models, resulting in an enormous number of potential solutions and growing the computational complexity of finding the optimum response. The computational complexity of centralized controllers' stymies IaaS adoption, especially for applications that need QoS guarantees and are responsive to user perceptions of latency, such as video streaming (Wuhib, 2013). Additionally, by integrating heuristic algorithms into centralized models running on a wide scale, the problem space is limited in one or more dimensions, allowing for effective heuristics at the expense of optimality.

As such, clustered resource allocation approaches are impractical and ineffective in geographically diverse and dynamic environments, an issue that persists. These disadvantages highlight the need for a fully autonomous solution to resource distribution that is not reliant on a central controller and makes efficient use of the distributed architecture (Lewis, 2014). There is a scalability concern involved with the computational sophistication challenge inherent in clustered approaches, which expresses itself by the presence of large numbers of constraints and variables. This well-known NP-Hard dilemma motivates this study to suggest a decentralized solution capable of rapidly reacting to the ever-changing circumstances associated with a very large number of requests/resources at a fine-grained level and within a realistic period.

3.3 Contributions of Cluster-Based Framework

The following highlights the work's contributions:

This thesis proposes a cluster-based architecture for geo-datacenters that span the globe and are organized into a collection of clusters, each of which is independently governed and managed by an elected cluster Coordinator. A Key CSP administrator manages the design, which includes defining the geographical limits of each cluster, the number of data centers, and the average pricing for each clustered resource. Geo-datacenter implemented in dispersed clusters guarantee network stability and resource availability in distant areas. Furthermore, this distributed deployment improves the number of permitted IaaS requests and the efficiency of supplied infrastructures.

This thesis offers two decentralized resource allocation methods to address the insufficiency and inefficiency of centralized resource allocation approaches in terms of scalability and analytical complexity. The large-scale resource distribution issue, in particular, introduces numerical complexity and impairs the efficiency of running programs. Economic models are offered as potential answers to the performance of resource use. With the Key CSP, we sought to reduce computing time and backbone network traffic. The following techniques are suggested: - A methodical approach to resource sharing. This approach utilizes a two-sided auction architecture to distribute incoming IaaS requests across Cluster-Coordinators following the CSP's gain in each cluster. As a result, the algorithm's numerical complexity is reduced. The Double-Sided auction incentivizes consumers to demonstrate their willingness to pay for desired infrastructures based on favorable factors such as price and efficiency. – A distributed resource management mechanism that collaborates with Cluster Coordinators via a Single-Round Sealed-Bid auction mechanism. This strategy incentivizes CSP's partners (i.e., Cluster Coordinators) to compete for high-quality resources to benefit CSP.

3.4 The Architecture and Essential Steps of Proposed Framework

In this section, the thesis proposes a cluster-based architecture capable of hosting any large application with stringent quality of service requirements.

The master stakeholder, the IaaS user, manages a diverse set of dispersed apps and wants to ensure their hosting. The second stakeholder, the Cloud Service Provider (CSP), is in charge of the clustered architecture and is accountable for providing a reliable platform that meets customer expectations.

The Thesis proposes an architecture that comprises multiple Data Centers distributed geographically and grouped to form clusters. The Data Centers are linked through a backbone network that is managed and maintained by the same Cloud Service Provider (CSP).

The proposed architecture's Data Centers and clusters are shown in Figure 1. (For example, east, west, north, and south).

There are two main organizations defined: a centralized Master Cloud Service Provider (CSP) and a selection of Cluster Coordinators (CCs) that service the clusters at the Master Cloud Service Provider's upper-stage decision-making level (CSP). Every x day, the extended cluster election process chooses at random the data center with the highest resource usage in the cluster.

Each CC member gets services and may decide whether to allocate suitable resources locally (distributed) or to the master cloud service provider (decentralized method) (hierarchical approach). To address any resource distribution problems that may occur as a consequence of restrictions, the controller may receive real-time information from the Master CSP (e.g., resource outages or user position).

Virtualization of physical servers (through partitioning) results in the creation of a collection of Virtual Clusters (VCs) or Virtual Machines (VMs) that conform to distinct Quality of Service (QoS) groups (Charles Reiss, 2011). In cluster c, the capability of VRs from QoS class q is defined as the total number of VRs available in the cluster resource pool, indicated by Cgq. The capacity of all intra data centers, where we take the maximum bandwidth available inside each cluster (v max) and then redistribute it across the c data centers to get the maximum aggregate (Bc) value (Al-Fares, 2008). The technique of "multiplexing" bandwidth on a single port enables the transmission of information between multiple computers. Unfortunately, ports are seldom used at full capacity for an extended length of time, and as a result, several smaller computers may share the same port to take advantage of the extra bandwidth when it is required (Al-Fares, 2008).

As long as one host on the network has the complete capacity of doing so, any computer on the network may interact with that host. Numerous data center designs include greater capacity as a cost-cutting strategy. Often, conventional Data Center networks are linked at least twice as fast as each other, resulting in each server in the Data Center being twice as sluggish as the one next to it. Creating a virtual capital pool whose growth spans all business divisions as well as inside and outside Data Centers entails two separate tasks: identifying and adding all Cluster-Virtual-Resources (Vc).

Ik = (Vk; Bk; Pk) indicates the number of virtual machines (VMs) required, with each VM having its own CPU, memory, and storage needs. Bk indicates the required bandwidth between two virtual machines, and Pk denotes the price that consumers are willing to pay.

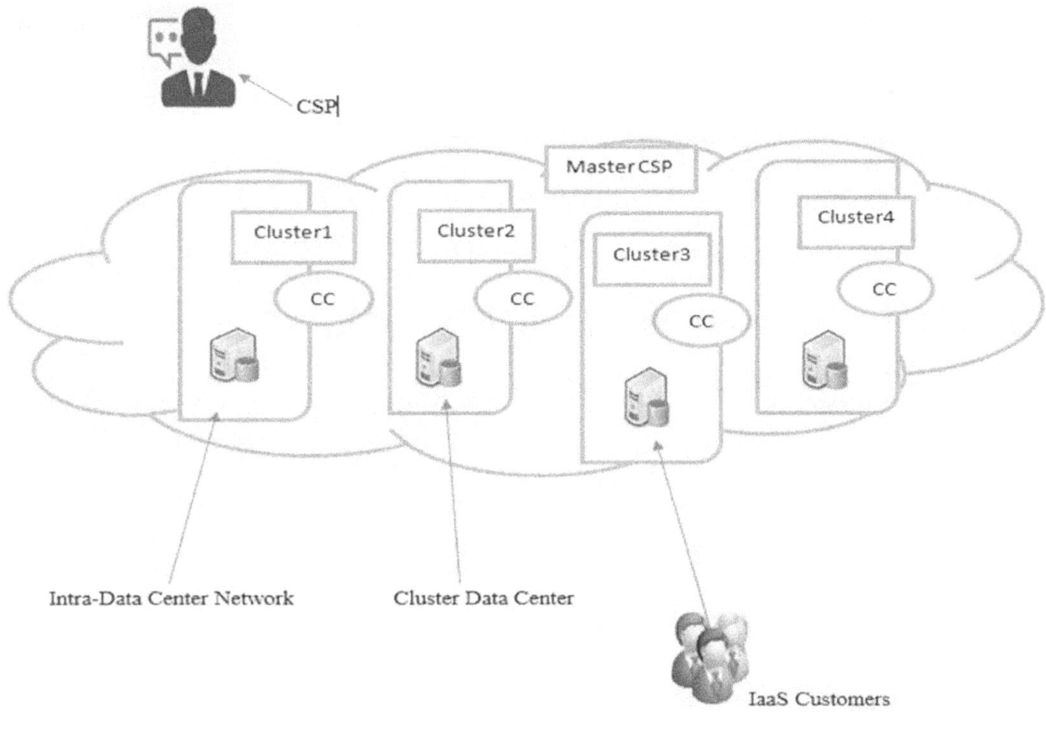

Figure 3.1: Proposed Cluster-based Framework

3.5 Clustered IaaS-Provisioning Algorithm

A cluster-based method capable of deploying any large-scale application with stringent quality of service requirements. The primary collaborator, the infrastructure-as-a-service client, has widely dispersed applications and requires a secure infrastructure to host them. The second partner, the Cloud Service Provider, owns the cluster dispersed method and is responsible for ensuring that the security framework is flexible enough to accept customer appeals. The framework's propound planning comprises of a diverse array of Data Centers located in a variety of geological regions and organized in batch-creating clusters. The assets at the knowledge center's heart are purchased and maintained by a persistent cloud service provider (Gupta, 2019).

We developed a clustered IaaS provisioning method in which Cluster Coordinators (CCs) operate independently of one another. The strategy is now horizontal, and the top cloud service provider is not involved. As a result, each CC strengthens its tasks as a self-seeking operation while also contributing a bit to others.

Algorithm for Clustered IaaS Provisioning:

- Data In: Bunch of M (Infrastructure-as-a-service) IaaS Requests, I_m = (Rm, Km, Bm),
- A set of Q Cloud Coordinators, $C_q = (C_v^q, B_a^q, P_v^q, P_l^q)$
- Data Out: Allocation of received (Infrastructure-as-a-service) IaaS requests to CCs, $S_{m,q}$
- Steps:
- Sort M Bids B1≥B2≥B3, ..., ≥BM
- Sort Q Prices $C_v^1 \leq C_v^2 \leq C_v^3 \leq C_v^4 \ldots \leq C_v^Q$
- m←0
- while (m≤M) do
- for each $C_q \in Q$ do
- if $C_v^q -$ Rm ≥ 0 and $B_a^q -$ Km ≥ 0 then
- Received← Received + 1
- $C_v^q \leftarrow C_v^q - R_m$
- $B_a^q \leftarrow B_a^q - K_m$
- $S_{m,q} \leftarrow (m, q)$
- Assigned←true
- m← m + one
- break
- end if

- end for
- if (! Assigned) then
- Assigned ←false
- Dismissed← Dismissed + one
- m←m + one
- end if
- end while

METHOD ALGO. 2: ALLOCATION 1: REPORT THE VENDUE

- Data In: Bunch of M Dismissed Infrastructure-as-a-Service Appeals, I_m = (Rm; Km; Bm)
- Data Out: Allocation of Dismissed (Infrastructure-as-a-service) IaaS appeals to Q Cloud Coordinators, $S_{m, q}$
- Report vendue by putting the dismissed appeals in a splitted accessible regions.
- Assemble the arriving offers from every cluster in $B_{m, q}$.
- Integrate the arriving offers into 1 record $L_{m, q} \leftarrow B_{m, q}$.
- Sort $L_{m, q}$ in descending order.
- for each (I_m) in (M) do
- if m = $L_{m, q}$ and $L_{m, q} >$ Zero then
- Set $S_{m, q} \leftarrow$ one
- Continue
- end if
- end for
- Broadcast $S_{m, q}$ to all the winning clusters

ALGORITHM DESCRIPTION

CCs to achieve the common objective of increasing the major CSP's total profitability. This clustered-based method mitigates the disadvantages of both centralized and distributed systems and significantly lowers both operating time and traffic in the n/w.

To begin, each Cluster Coordinator (CC) collects Infrastructure-as-a-Service (IaaS) requests that are approved in their cluster. Following that, each group allocates adequate resources to such appeals on its own. When CCs bidding on requests are reported, the modification takes effect. Meanwhile, each responds to other CCs' reports by putting bids on them.

CCs that have been announced begin gathering offers from other participants, evaluating them, and choosing the most viable proposals. Following that, rejected pleas are sent to vanquishing groups and shown during the following round of resource allocation.

MECHANISM OF SINGLE-SIDED AUCTION

The following stages describe the functional systematic procedure:

- Each cluster should provide the first phase of IaaS using the regional resource allocation methodology.
- Implement inherent benefits of Cloud Service Provider in every cluster separately.
- Implement a single-party vendue system (dismissed appeals) as follows:
- If (Dismissed appeals are available)

  Do assignment 1.
- If (report found in a shared cluster)

  Then do Assignment 2.
- Distribute assignment results to auction participants.
- Upon request from other groups as a result of the auction, adopt the Regional Resource

allocation (RCG-IaaS) model and perform a second round of cluster-based IAAS.

- Calculate the additional benefit of Cloud Service Provider in each group.

METHOD ALGO. 3: ALLOCATION 2: ORGANIZE THE VENDUE

- Data In: Bunch of M Dismissed (Infrastructure-as-a-service) IaaS Request, I_m = (Rm; Km; Bm)
- Data Out: Bid Record O_q
- while true do
- Assemble reported dismissed appeals on J_q.
- Classify J_q in decreasing order.
- if size $(J_q) \geq$is Zero then
- for each (I_m) in J_q do
- if (C_v^q $-R_m \geq$Zero) and B_a^q $-K_m \geq$Zero then
- $C_v^q \leftarrow C_v^q - R_m$
- $B_v^q \leftarrow B_v^q - K_m$
- Calculate B_m
- $O_q \leftarrow B_m$
- Else
- $O_q \leftarrow$Zero
- end if
- end for
- end if
- Broadcast O_q for remaining contributors
- end while

ALGORITHM DESCRIPTION

The vendue method ensures stability in the provision of infrastructure-as-a-service by preventing recurrence and announcing just one winner. The second and third algorithms describe the practical activities involved with the transition to a cluster-based approach: (1) tracking bidding activity; and (2) managing bids.

These assignments work similarly inside each CC's two running strings. The primary watches bartering for excused solicitations, while the secondary checks other members' closeout reports.

When forgivable requests are received, the primary task specified in calculation 2 is executed after the first stage. CC is now advertising a deal on a well-known publicly accessible domain and seeking bids from other members (line three). After accumulating all approaching deals (lines four and five), it classifies them as plunging requests (line six) and selects the best-enhanced offer that maximizes the CSP's overall profit. Attempts with a low intrinsic value are permitted (lines seven-twelve).

A solicitation is void if the offer is less than Sm, q 0, or if the offer does not exist at the time the solicitation is made. Furthermore, the calculation is expanded to include the following solicitation. Each CC then begins presenting its argument to the winning factions (line thirteen).

Calculation three executes the matching task, which listens for any reported shared area sales (line three). Each CC keeps track of all excused requests in the common area Jq (line four) and defers canceled requests while forwarding non-refundable ones (line five).

Additionally, CC checks the availability of assets for each request and, if sufficient assets are available, creates a new concept to meet that requirement. Otherwise, it is set to 0. (Lines 7–

16). The first Oq. does not include the findings.

The CC starts grouping rundown Oq and alerting various Oq collecting participants (line eighteen). Each CC advances to the second stage when authorized agreements are in place.

3.6 IaaS Provisioning Architecture

Tropically, the bidder is a failure. Extra value administrators will magnify their requirements and underutilized resources, amassing additional surplus to assist meet the demands of future IaaS-based growth, resulting in an increase in net revenue (Zaman and Grosu, 2010). To reduce, one solution is to vary the sale time frame's recurrence. Because IaaS items may be classified as different services, they are divided into assemblies, each of which is tuned to a particular length of time. Solicitors are not scared of the cost required to get more customers [clients and money are less of a concern to them]. Professors and students at the institution are aware that if their fortunes change, they will be offered another opportunity to conduct further transactions. A second agreement among the customer community that constitutes a conspiracy against the Cloud Service Provider comes when they submit a bid that is identical to that submitted by others who conspire together (Quttoum, 2010). Cloud Service Provider has no other option than to award the assets to those bidders, posing a severe threat to revenue. To avoid agreement, CSPs may define a base selling price by updating the number of assets based on the historical context of previous closeouts.

Additionally, our proposal makes use of sell-offs to achieve coordination between Master CSPs and CCs. Our approach enables each autonomous CC to tailor its evaluation to management imperatives such as electricity costs. Although our engineering is managed and overseen by the same CSP (Main CSP and CCs), we designed our decentralized estimates around the concept of a closeout that maintains a strategic gap between fixed costs and participant benefits, as shown below.

- The strategy's many phases are organized using a two-sided auction mechanism.
- A one-sided oversupply component: utilized in the scattered technique as a flat coordinating mechanism among CCs.

DECENTRALIZED PROVISIONING APPROACHES

At the moment, illustrate our two decentralized methods (various leveled and appropriated). The multi-leveled method is dependent on two-level vertical coordination. The scattered approach achieves comparable coordination across different controllers (i.e., CCs), allowing for effective and autonomous asset allocation. Additionally, we propose a Hierarchical-Cluster Infrastructure-as-a-Service providing Architecture (HCIA) based on a streamlined disintegration process called Column Generation (CG) (Ubbecke and Desrosiers, 2005).

DISTRIBUTED IaaS PROVISIONING

CCs act independently in the communicated Infrastructure-as-a-Service-provisioning method. Thus, coordination is even, without the Master _Cloud Service Provider's involvement.

As a result, each CC develops its distributions independently, while collaborating with other CCs to achieve the common objective of enhancing the Master Cloud Service Provider's total benefit.

This tailored technique alleviates the drawbacks of the focused methodology by reducing both computation time and traffic on the spine arrangement.

To begin, each CC compiles the IaaS requirements that have been assigned to it. At that moment, each gathering is free to allocate the appropriate resources to those requests. The shift occurs when CCs announce a bartering agreement after dismissing cases. In the meantime, each CC's statements will be reacted to by placing its proposals. The designated CCs begin collecting offers from other members, evaluating their suggestions, and selecting the most profitable offer. In the second round, companies are chosen based on their desire in growing and get unrequested allocations of available money. The stages for adopting organizational advances are as follows:

Each cluster should complete the first step of Infrastructure-as-a-Service providing by implementing the Hierarchical-Cluster IaaS provisioning Architecture HCIA.

Implement the critical advantage of the Cloud Service Provider separately in each cluster.

Execute the single-side closeout component as follows (for rejected solicitations):

Carry out Task 1 if the event contains the denied request.

Carry out Task 2 if declarations on mutual clusters are discovered.

Distribute the findings to the appropriate auctioneers.

Implement the second step of Infrastructure-as-a-Service providing by obtaining the HCIA on solicitations issued by various bunches as a consequence of bartering.

Implement the additional advantage of the Cloud Service Provider in each cluster.

HIERARCHICAL IAAS PROVISIONING

Currently, are divided into two tiers, as shown in Figure 3.2. Although the main CSP is responsible for user authentication, the following group of CAs is also responsible for customer authentication. When we did so, we evaluated the benefits to each stakeholder group (Grover, 2007). Each cluster streamlines the surrounding view by using a productive IaaS provisioning strategy (HCIA). The global view objective is accomplished by using a two-sided sell-off to communicate the clustering utilization levels and estimate data with the progression's higher stage.

This method is capable of passing the numerical complexity examination. We divided the Main

CSP operation into two activities throughout the two phases. The main objective is to divide future IaaS needs across the bunches following the benefit calculated at each CC. It is considered a lightweight operation for complicated systems in which programs are spread across the main threads of the Main CSP controller (at level 1). The following job requires the establishment of strict processes for updating asset assignments in each bunch independently. This task is completed for each CC (at level 2). Expanding the arithmetic enables a lower limit and fewer constraints on the resource's dispersion techniques. By dividing the computation and maintenance load, controllers at the controller may quickly respond to unforeseen changes or fulfill requests in the unified controller, everything remains in one piece. Horizontal integration of these two activities is required for appropriate proficiency, much more so in a massive situation (Lee, 2015).

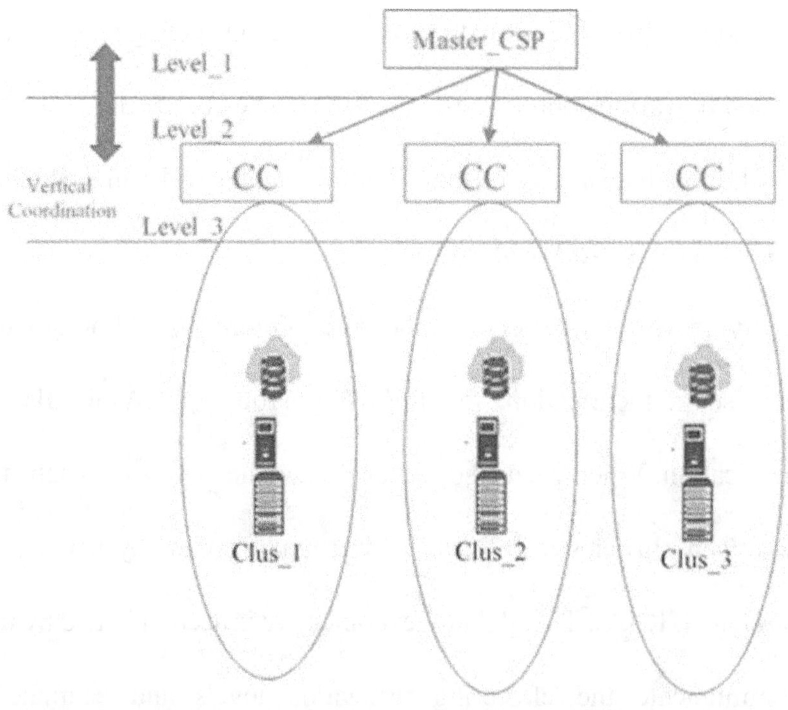

Figure 3.2: Proposed Hierarchical-Cluster IaaS provisioning Architecture (HCIA)

Within a two-sided sale, the customers' IaaS requirements are on one side, while the credit card charges are on the other. To guarantee consistent revenue monitoring, the Master Cloud Service Provider (CSP) searches for and records charges and information from customers' CCs and (mainly SaaS sales clients). Expanding to develop any guidelines for the subjects is a procedure that begins with getting a proposal from two subjects. The Master Cloud Service Provider (Master CSP) follows a rigorous process to assemble winning specifications for clients, offering a great value proposition to those who can supply maximum capacity and IaaS, and provisioning winning IaaS offerings for those who want the most. To be clear, we think that the closeout was done correctly. It is unethical to exaggerate or downplay the actual significance of a deal's conclusion. The CSP believes that regardless of who they are, they would help their clients and suppliers.

The Master Cloud service provider then distributes the IaaS requests across the victorious CCs to maximize the advantages. Finally, each CC starts providing for the set of solicitations received locally in its lot. Calculation one starts by classifying approaching IaaS needs based on submitted offers in sliding requests (line five), sorting the prices supplied by credit card companies in increasing requests (line six), and comparing the solicitations to the costs. The metric validates the applicability of each property in the comparison category (line ten). If it has sufficient assistance, the coordination process is complete, and the request is assigned to that group (lines 11-17). Before this phase, the case is attached and the speculative cost and benefit are calculated, but no assets have been allocated. These methods are rehashed for every upcoming request. Solicitations involving bombed designations are deemed null and void (lines 20-23). The estimate produces a task list (Sn, g) including approved requests and potential clusters for allocation. The Master CSP, in his capacity as the barker, begins by declaring matches between winning cases and winning parties and then distributes solicitations to specific groups.

After completing the lightweight assignment of the two-sided side sale, the progressive approach moves on to the heavyweight assignment, which is the asset allocation in each group using the HCIA. Each CC meets its assigned requirements and distributes the appropriate assets to increase its revenue.

EXPERIMENTAL SETUP

We are now showing the test setup with different parameters that were previously described. To compare the proposed decentralized system's capability to current benchmarks, we evaluated an adequate network of 16 Data Centers distributed throughout India in four different clusters: East, West, and two clusters in the Middle, as shown in Figure 3.1. Each bunch is comprised of four Data Centers, each of which includes an indefinite number of VMs with different degrees of granularity according to Google Quality of Service groups (Charles Reiss, 2011). Additionally, each data center makes use of a well-known device architecture (for example, FatTree) and an aggregated estimate of intra-Data Center system transfer speed based on different oversubscription esteems, as stated in (M. Al-Fares, 2008). The dispersed data centers are linked through the NSFNet topology, which acts as a backbone organization segmented into the required bunches (National Science Foundation Network, 2015). Each data center is connected to the NSFNet through the hub located closest to its location. We concur that all NSFNet connections have a comparable bandwidth limit of 10Gbps. IaaS needs are generated using a C++ traffic generator module inspired by GT-ITM (Zegura and Bhattacharjee, 1996). The number of VMs allocated per demand is constantly between three and fifteen. Additionally, the required assets in each VM and the associated data transfer capacity requirement across VMs are evenly distributed between 300Mbps and 1Gbps.

The outstanding obligations are produced regularly between 50 and 100 solicitations for small estimated IaaS remaining burdens with standard 300 VM and 500 association and between 120 and 200 solicitations for enormous approximate remaining burdens with standard 1700 VM and 1200 association. We used a cyclical strategy (Jarray and A. Karmouch, 2012). The preparatory period for re-enactment is divided into many stages p P. The cycle is adaptable in order to minimize the distortions inherent in sales and is characterized by an unusually large number of solicitations gathered in tiny groupings. This method for dispensing periodic tiny clusters is as follows: Assume that P represents the arrangement of arrangement cycles and that R (0) represents the underlying arrangement of IaaS specifications. The following diagram depicts the Organisation of IaaS requirements R(p) as defined by p1:

"R(p) = R (p − 1) + Rnew(p) − Rdrop(p)"

where "R (p 1)" denotes the arrangement of recognized IaaS requirements at the end of cycle "p-1. Rnew(p)" represents the arrangement of novel methods, while "Rdrop(p)" represents the arrangement of consummation IaaS requirements at the start of cycle p. The approach replicates a real-world cloud environment and enables the evaluation of the model's productivity in the face of an explosion in IaaS demand.

It is beneficial to conduct testing in immersed working circumstances to more easily evaluate the exhibition of IaaS provisioning methods. During routine system operation, joins are often provisioned to 30% to 50% of their capabilities (Jain, 2013). As a result, the solicitation generator is triggered, flooding the system with solicitations. We next conduct testing for 10 consecutive periods and record all installation results. This process is repeated many times, and natural characteristics are investigated. To demonstrate the methodology's flexibility, we increase the number of IaaS requests from one to one hundred. We repeat this method many times and use the expected results.

The games are performed using our C++-based discrete event test framework. We do extensive simulations using a variety of factors, including the number of IaaS requests, the number of clusters, the number of Data Centers in each group, and various oversubscription esteem. The queries were performed on an HP machine equipped with a 2.3 GHz Intel Core 5 CPU and 8 GB of RAM that was configured to run Windows 10 home single language and the IBM CPLEX solver (IBM LOG CPLEX Optimizer, 2015).

PERFORMANCE EVALUATION METRICS

We utilized the following exhibition measures to compare the presentation of Hierarchical-Cluster IaaS provisioning Architecture (HCIA) and Two-stage IaaS heuristic provisioning methods:

Acceptance proportion: at each point in time, the ratio of recognized IaaS solicitations to all filed applications.

DC asset utilization: the proportion of properties (CPU, memory, stockpiling, and transfer speed) that are fully used in the DC.

The CSP's net value is equal to the aggregate value of the benefits received by each cluster coordinator (CC) in each category. The benefit is calculated by the offers collected via successful solicitations, minus the cost of system assets and the model-derived VMs.

A critical performance measure:

Speedup (Su): Acceleration is achieved by using several preparatory hubs rather than a single hub.

Efficiency (E): Percentage of maximum potential execution (acceleration or utilization) (percent)

Elasticity (El): Dynamic interim control of auto-scaling characteristics while maintaining load variety

Cloud-based Productivity:

Cloud QoS: The pace at which cloud management or benchmark monitoring job is completed (percent)

Service Price: The cost of each cloud management service (Computing, Storage, and so on.) has been specified ($/hour).

Availability (A): The proportion of time that the system is available to perform relevant tasks.

SIMULATION SCENARIOS

Productivity gains from IaaS provisioning: Hierarchical-Cluster IaaS Provisioning Architecture (HCIA) vs. Two-stage heuristic approach

At the moment, the suggested Hierarchical-Cluster Infrastructure as a Service providing Architecture (HCIA) is being compared to the writing's Two-stage hub and connection heuristic provisioning estimate. It considers the use of Geo-Data Center services, the financial advantages of CSPs, and the recognition of IaaS clients. To assess our model's effectiveness, we utilized the following benchmarks.

Network-Aware Architecture as a Service Provisioning in Distributed Clouds (NA-RA): This concept used a two-stage computation of IaaS asset components (Phase 1: identifies the Data Centers/servers to which IaaS hubs (VMs) should be attached, and Stage 2: identifies the servers to link) (VMs). For the usage of dispersed mists and consideration of dispersion while determining sub-charts.

RCG-IaaS provisioning of Geographically Dispersed Clouds (Khaled Metwally, 2018): This concept envisions the basic cloud computing paradigm operating on a decentralized scale, with numerous data centers connected through a backbone.

We received a variety of outstanding work sets including IaaS specifications for roughly 1900 virtual machines and 1400 associations with clear criteria.

Figures 3.3(c) and 3.3(d) compare the financial advantages of the Hierarchical-Cluster IaaS Architecture (HCIA) to the two benchmark configurations (NA-RA, RCG-IaaS) in terms of acknowledgment percentage and net profit. As expected, Figures 3.3(a) and 3.3(b) show that the proposed HCIA outperforms other structures in terms of IaaS recognition percentage, profit, and Geo-Data Center asset utilization (CPU and spine BW). This is mainly proven by the method of implanting a single hub and link and the effective use of CG as a wide scope advancement device. One-shot implanting enables greater coordination between the IaaS hub and connection mapping, which results in a higher IaaS acknowledgment percentage as compared to two-stage inserting. The use of CG eliminates the inherent trade-off between bury and intra-Data Center transmission capacity expenses. The results obtained from the n spine arrange usage, Figure 3.3(b), showed that the Hierarchical-Cluster IaaS Architecture (HCIA) made the best use of intra-transmission capacity to serve the incoming solicitations first. Due to a blackout of an asset (i.e., intra-transmission capacity), the model reaches out to simulate the distribution using the between-Data Center transfer rate. NA-RA execution values are comparable to our model. NA-RA has a similar objective of limiting conveyance in the spine arrangement via the use of charts. Figures 3.3(g) and 3.3(h) illustrate the flexibility and Quality of Services (QoS) of RCG-IaaS, Na-Ra, and HCIA, respectively. The HCIA is much more competent in working and providing a variety of sorts of support at server farms, as well as providing excellent QoS, among three. Figures 3.3(i) and 3.3(j) depict the expense and accessibility of administrations in the customers' best interest at different data centers. There is a significant improvement in HCIA when compared to the two methods (RCG-IaaS, NA-RA).

The adaptability of infrastructure-as-a-service provisioning: reconciled centralized and decentralized methods

To determine the adaptability of decentralized methods, we used an integrated model (K. M. Metwally, 2015) as a benchmark.

We evaluated the design's flexibility by seeing how it responded when the outstanding tasks at hand were increased. We discovered that CSPs' economic benefits increased.

The tests confirmed the significant increase in productivity, as shown in Figures 3.3(e) and 3.3. (f). The HCIA method is unmatched in that it provides an additional distribution channel. This additional open door increases the acknowledgment percentage and the net benefit, at the price of a little higher cost. Additionally, regardless of the global viewpoint on part in the, RCG-IaaS the different leveled method and HCIA the Hierarchical-Cluster IaaS provisioning architecture execute in an obscenely short time. This reaffirms the applicability of closeout strategies in decentralized methods.

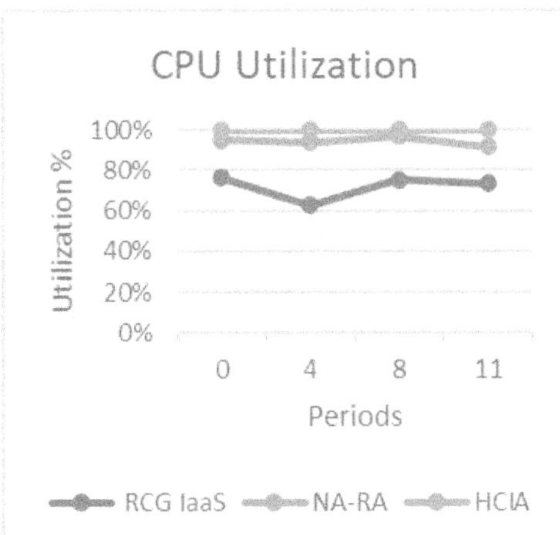

3.3(a)

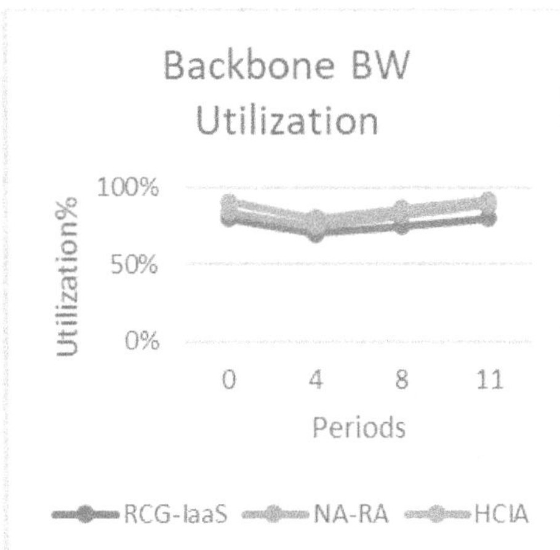

3.3(b)

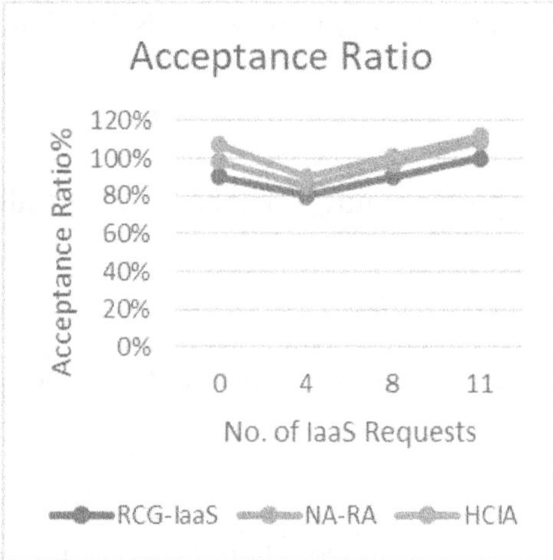

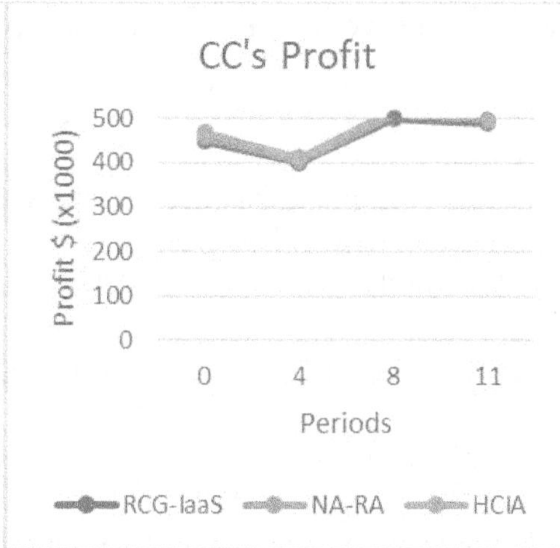

3.3 (c)

3.3 (d)

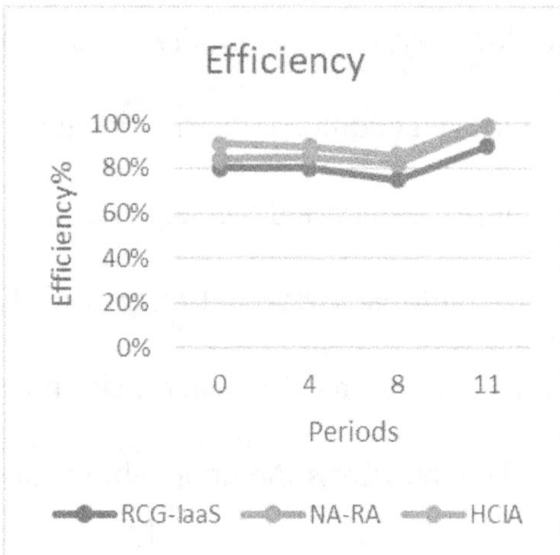

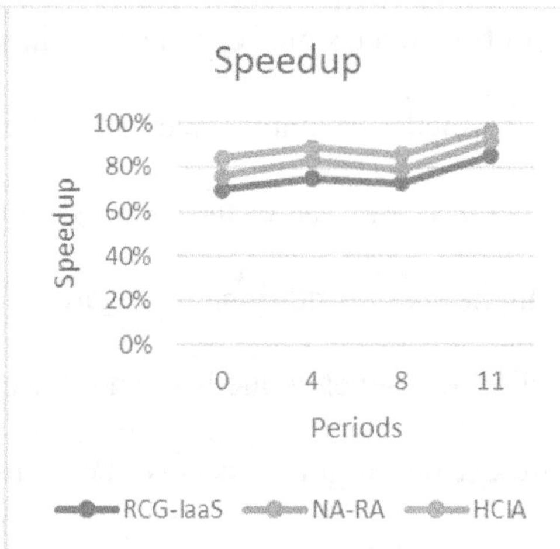

3.3 (e)

3.3 (f)

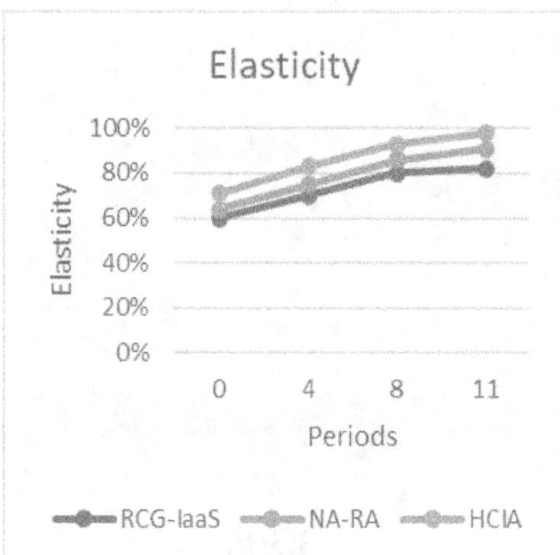

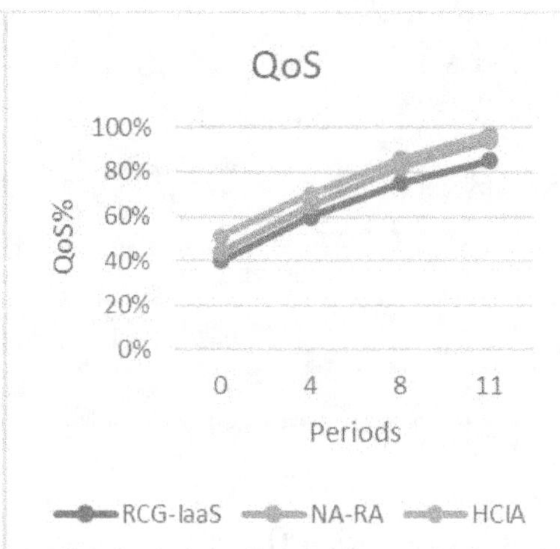

3.3 (g)

3.3 (h)

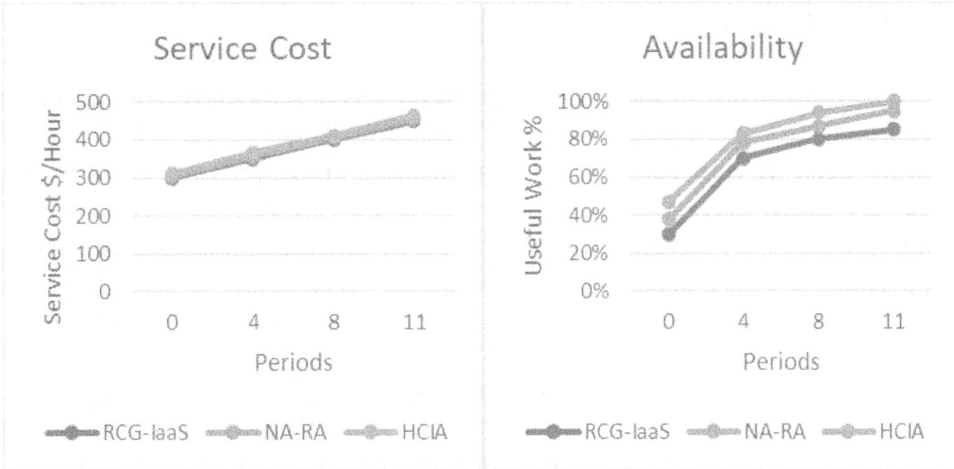

3.3 (i) **3.3 (j)**

Figure 3.3: Simulation Scenarios of Different Parameters

3.7 Summary

The method to IaaS provisioning HCIA stated that the entire IaaS provisioning is dynamic and places a greater focus on other performance criteria such as elasticity, quality of service, service cost, and availability, achieving a higher level than the previous two methods (RCG-IaaS, and NA-RA). As a result, the HCIA technique outperforms all other described approaches.

Chapter 4: 4.1 Introduction

Despite these obstacles, huge data centers become economically inefficient as their costs increase in lockstep with the development of continuing large-scale application demands. Currently, the study has developed a framework for Infrastructure-as-a-Service arrangements that guarantee a cost-effective, flexible, and quality-of-service-assured method for soliciting large expansions in geographically distributed data centers. The structure joins two scattered methodological divisions that are near, distinct, progressive, and communicated, and that make effective use of monetary representations. There are many approaches, each having an incredibly positive response to the adaptability and calculability of the current ways multifarious character. Finally, cost efficiency has been connected to a distributed structure that is suitable in light of the extra constraints influencing Cloud Service Provider benefits. Preoccupation yields show the offer's efficiency by comparing the prospective profits of provided courses of action to the customers' needs, all while attaining exceptional resource utilization and Cloud Service Provider (CSP) payoffs. Additionally, the thesis suggested a resource allocation method based on clustering. The thesis integrates the Vickrey-Clarke-Groves (VCG) system to improve understanding of intrigue and misrepresentation in a cluster-distributed resource allocation method using geo-distributed datacenters. Additionally, the study will illustrate this via simulation, which will pit many bids against one another for a big contract. Numerous responsibilities are included in the contract. Certain jobs must be outsourced due to their essential nature. Others are not essential and, if left unassigned, incur a penalty. The goal is to determine the most cost-effective method of assigning work to bidders. Thus, no collusion between those bidders is permitted throughout the bidding process.

VCG components, in particular, are not completely immune to group strategy. If we want to utilize a VCG variable in a situation where operators may interfere, it is critical to examine which bosses may successfully coordinate to undermine the system and under what conditions this may occur. This is self-evident for some basic Vickrey-Clarke-Grove arrangements, such as the Vickrey sale with a single item. Regardless, the mechanics of collecting controls using different methods are considerably more complex. (Archer, 2004).

Consider that a VCG closeout is completely performed online and that a single bidder may participate in the sale under several screen identities. Assume that verifying that different screen names correspond to distinct bids is impossible. A shill offering is recognized with permission. Without the internet, shill offers will emerge if a single leader outbids many other bidders. Additionally, investigations into specific misleading techniques have started. (Sakurai, 1999)

The following example demonstrates how a shill offering may be justified. Locate two bidders, Rony and Tom, as well as two pieces of goods, 1 and 2. Influence rates a single item that is more expensive than the average at $1, and the category that includes all products that are more expensive than the average at $4. Rony values each spectacular at $1.50 and the party at $3. Giving the pack to Tom is a really powerful gesture. Under a legitimate bid, the VCG part of the community is provided to Tom for $3. Apart from that, Rony will attend the auction as two different individuals, Clark and John. Hymn says that only a great 1 is worth $3.50, and John affirms that only a great 2 is worth $3.50; confident in these bargains, it is justifiable to reward Clark with a great 1 and John with a great 2. Rony will now get the two items. Tune's VCG contribution will be $1 = $4.50 $3.50. If Clark is barred from bidding, $4.50 acts as a powerful incentive for all bidders: John will really win magnificent 2, while Tom will win great 1. $3.50 has established itself as a driving factor for John and Tom in their lucrative task, which includes Clark. Using almost equal logic, John's VCG part will therefore be $1. Due to the reality that Rony is liable for the parts of each piece offered by his seller bidders, Rony's finished portion is $2. Since Rony obtains both products, his utility is 3-2 = 1, which is greater than his utility from genuine participation, which is void. The rule problem is that when a seller offers, the pioneer never considers a single bidder again. The VCG framework's concept is that each manager is responsible for his externality. Regardless, it is difficult to perceive the boss again when a shill bid is made.

Shill's proposal is associated with suspense on a personal level. Leaving aside the conventional motivation to stifle competition, the disincentive to collapse using shills when confronted with a comparable valuation transforms into an urge to unite with a coalition when confronted with a comparable valuation. (Sher. Itai, 2009)

We demonstrate the implementation of the VCG mechanism in this segment, which resolves the issue of collusion in the allocation of bidders to bids through geo-distributed data centers. Then, the specification and application of a series of operational measures for disseminating assessments outcomes.

A combinatorial auction is exemplified by the VCG Mechanism. A bid is a valuation in the VCG Process. The VCG process then allocates resources efficiently, accepting the offers at face value. That is, products are spread among bidders in such a way that the number of recorded valuations is maximized. (Shashi Kant, Gupta, 2019)

We are currently faced with the task of resolving the problem of exaggeration and collusion in the cloud system, where we are distributing different resources to IaaS consumers through a cluster-distributed approach of resource allocation.

Given the possibility that bidder partnerships may sometimes collude to deceive the VCG portion, it is important to understand which meetings may successfully attract and under what conditions these possibilities occur. We examine these issues in the context of a hotly contested topic known as multicast bid collecting (A. Archer, 2003).

At the moment, a basic and instinctive condition applicable to lone competitors indicates whether or not insufficiencies exist. In a competitive setting where each opponent exhibits substitutional tendencies, the aforementioned disadvantage would never exist. In either case, if there is a single bidder whose tendencies are detrimental to the substitute's situation, then the entirety of the above inadequacies would be available with a fair assessment of characteristics for the remaining bidders (whether or not the final characteristics are retained as substance).

Evaluations of the VCG mechanism often overlook the trading profits. This is a magnificent evasion. A single vendor's life is critical. Without a doubt, as the organization accelerates, internal needs such as allocating profitability, promoting ownership by privately held businesses or women or minority-led associations, compensating growth, and preserving a vital good way from centralized ownership are critical considerations, one of the introductions checks frequently emphasized by individuals (Itai Sher, 2012).

On a more fundamental level, it's especially troubling because Vickrey closeout tasks may be very restricted or even non-existent, despite the fact that the goods being auctioned are rather basic and disagreement is acceptable. Consider the hypothetical situation in which two territorial licences are revoked from three competitors. Assume rival 1 requires a maximum of two licences and is willing to pay $4 billion, while competitors 2 and 3 only need a single grant and are willing to pay $4 billion. The V.C.G method distributes permits to competitors

2 and 3 properly. According to the remaining competitors, the amount paid by competitor 2 qualifies him for one grant or two permits. Because the spacing is zero, the cost is also nil! A similar end was spent in the same manner as rival 3, indicating that the opportunities for rough and simple contract work are non-existent.

For example, had the firm sold the two licences individually at the time, it would have drawn three competitors ready to pay $4 billion for the combined award. To begin, there is much debate: a rising closeout may have required a $4 billion expense. The clear absence of recommended pay in the VCG framework supports its use in a broad range of practical implementations.

Pay reliability in the absence of the Vickrey closeout refers to the retailer's inability to receive in one manner or another as a result of rivals' conduct and the overall bid. Whether the third competitor is removed or its incentive for obtaining a permit is reduced from $4 billion to zero, the vendor's salaries in the V.C.G. contract will increase from $0 to $4 billion under the prior model. This inconsistency is not just a possible marketing problem; it often results in the creation of conditions and bugs that bidders can sometimes exploit.

Due to the passive nature of the Vickrey method, it is difficult to implement, even with losing bidders. This is shown in a variation of the preceding model; in which competitor 1's characteristics are preserved but competitors 2 and 3's qualities are diminished to the point that each can pay just $0.5 billion for a single permit. The change in merit essentially eliminates competitors 2 and 3 from the closeout. Bear in mind, however, that if each competitor pays $2 billion (bn) for their distinct qualities, the result will be similar to or more than: everyone will get one permit for free! It seems as if the V.C.G. component is so vulnerable that deprived competitors would engage in constructive linked divergence, thus enabling selling compromise.

The closely related scheme is a variant on shill offering (bidding), a term that alludes to a competitor's employment of several identities during the closeout process. To construct this model, let us replace competitors 2 and 3 with a single unified rival with characteristics of \$1 billion for a single permission and \$2 billion for a portfolio of permits. Again, the qualifying portion assigns licences to rival 1, ensuring that the combined competitor cannot succeed. If the barker is unable to ascertain the actual names of the competitors, the combined applicant may conduct the closeout under the guises of "competitor 2" and "competitor 3," each of which offers \$2 billion for a single permit. As previously stated, rivals 2 and 3 benefit without incurring any costs, indicating that the combined competitor benefits from all licences without incurring any costs.

A similar problem exists with the VCG system regardless of whether each rival flaunts their better methods, which are then followed by consensus or by different personalities. Assume once again that competitors 2 and 3 are individually worth \$4 billion for a single authorization, but that by merging their activities, the package's value increases from \$8 billion to \$8+X billion. If both competitors provide their valuations in the manner specified in the original Vickrey inquiry, then broken competitors 2 and 3 will pay nothing and will benefit cumulatively by \$4 billion. Prior to the haggling, combining competitors 2 and 3 would raise the cost from zero to \$2 billion, causing the businesses to think that combining is only lucrative if X>\$2 billion. Thus, although the dominating process framework of the VCG mechanism provides the optimal driving force for offering with a predetermined arrangement of bids, it distorts pre-closeout options associated with merging rivals. Take notice that in each of these models, competitor 1 values the whole bundle.

If we change the guidelines to give competitor 1 with permit replacements, for example, by determining that competitor 1 is willing to pay $1 billion for each permit rather than merely $2 billion for the pair, the whole of our judgements will vary. The merchant's total sales in the primary model will be $2 billion, a sizable sum in light of the result. This shift has an effect on the totality of the associated styles, the lucrative use of various characteristics in offerings, and the resistance to value-creating partnerships.

Reserve state ultimately comes across as authoritative in the Vickrey closeout's presentation. The end is developed via the frequent analysis that happens. We show that the above-mentioned kinds of issues cannot persist if each rival is forced to display substitution inclinations. Additionally, if applicable, competitor views contain additional material views; if this is not feasible owing to obvious substitute's trends; rival live views explain the extent of previously indicated issues.

4.2 Design and Implementation Phase: The Cluster-Distributed Resource-Allocation Approach

The proposal of a cluster-distributed resource allocation method is driven by Cluster Coordinators desire to operate independently of the Master Cloud Service Provider. Additionally, if the proposed design previously used concentrated models, the advantages and favorable conditions brought about by the communicated engineering may be clearly stated. Along these lines, suggesting an entirely appropriated asset distribution strategy right now that incorporates a bartering component as a coordinating mechanism. At the moment, coordination is handled entirely by free Cluster Coordinators, without the involvement of the Master Cloud Service Provider (Master CSP). Without using the Master CSP, Cluster-Coordinators make delivery choices, coordinate, and then reallocate. Participants may save money on communication expenses by using barters, since bids give their real reward in a single offer fixed value sell off (Chard, 2010).

In the proposed approach, each Cluster Coordinator reimagines its conveyances as a separate situation issue, but works together with other Cluster Coordinators to some degree in order to achieve the shared objective of raising the Master CSPs maximum scale profit. The distributed technique controller game-plan is shown in Figure: 4.1, in which all Cluster Coordinators coordinate uniformly through the backbone coordination arrangement. We argue that the approach clearly specifies the affirmation scope, shortens the mix time, eliminates task duplication, and ensures the benefit assignment phase's consistency. The proposed cluster-distributed resource allocation approach solution overcomes the constraints of the combined strategy based on a stunning general approach in terms of controlling the computational multifarious nature and sorting out the traffic on the backbone network. This method divides the calculation area into a large number of specified components capable of executing the basic estimates independently.

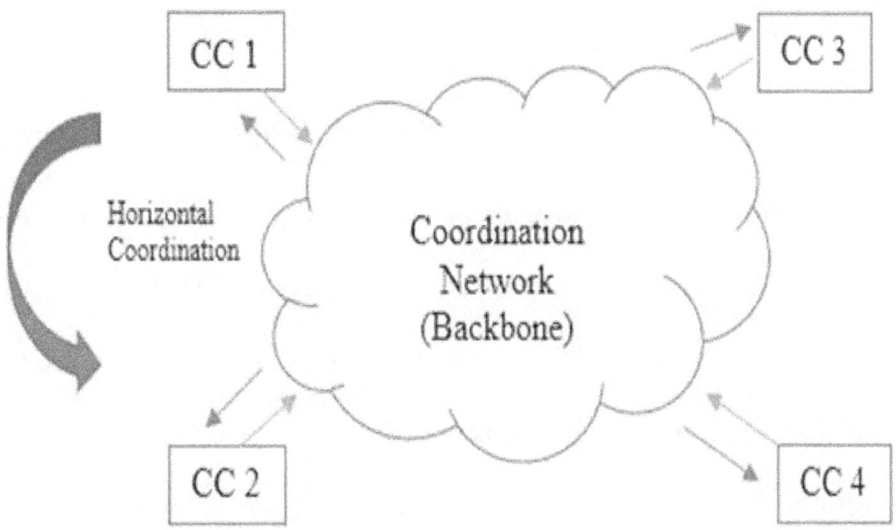

Figure 4.1: Proposed cluster-distributed resource-allocation approach

Well, known dispersed calculations are tested through 2 principal matters, computational time & stability of common information. The propound approach conquers these constraints with an effectiveness sell off system. The propound approach works by utilizing a solitary offer fixed value sell off component as a change among 2 cycles of resource allotment.

The functional strides of propound approach are abridged below:

Every locale, play out the first emphasis asset designation by receiving the regional resource allocation model.

2. Implement the Cloud Service Provider fundamental benefit in every area exclusively.

3. Run single-offer fixed value sell off mechanism (for dismissed solicitations) as follows:

(a.) If (Dismissed Appeals exist) Then Do Job 1

(b.) If (Found declarations on the mutual zone) Then

Do Job 2

(c) Communicate the project's outcomes to the deal's participants.

4. Perform a second cycle of territorial asset distribution by receiving regional resource allocation models based on solicitations provided by various clusters as a consequence of bartering.

5. Integrate the Cloud Service Provider advantage into each cluster.

The closeout mechanism progresses from the first to the following cycle by receiving a single offer fixed value sell-off component from Cluster Coordinators. This method achieves the optimal level coordination. Additionally, it is worth noting that Cloud Service Provider benefit is achieved by aggregating the calculated benefit in each focus. Correspondence between different Cluster Coordinators is facilitated by defining a common cluster as a result of each Cluster Coordinator having a one-of-a-kind identification. Systematization of the two assignments is critical for increasing the effectiveness of resource designation, particularly in large-scale conditions (C. Lee, 2015). To accomplish this efficiently, a vertical coordination has been accomplished by utilizing a two-tiered side sale component between the two progressive levels. The suggested method then repeats the first cycle, during which each Cluster Coordinator collects the IaaS requests received in its location (stage-1). After that, each location is free to manage the assets associated with the collected solicitations by using the RCG-IaaS model and calculating its profit (stage-2). Following the completion of the first cycle of asset allocation, each Cluster Coordinator checks for dismissed demands and reports a closeout if any exist by completing assignment (1) (step-3-a). During the interval, each Cluster Coordinator inspects for other members' declarations (that is, Cluster Coordinators) in mutual zone and responds to them by per-shaping assignment (2). (Step-3-b). At that time, Cluster Coordinator starts communicating to other members the outcomes of either assignment (1) or assignment (2). These assignment outcomes are referred to as the evaluation outputs for both accepting offers and establishing offers for existing declarations as a consequence of assignment (1) and assignment (2). (Step-3-c). At that point, the approach advances to the second focus on resource identification and final benefit calculations (stages-4 & 5).

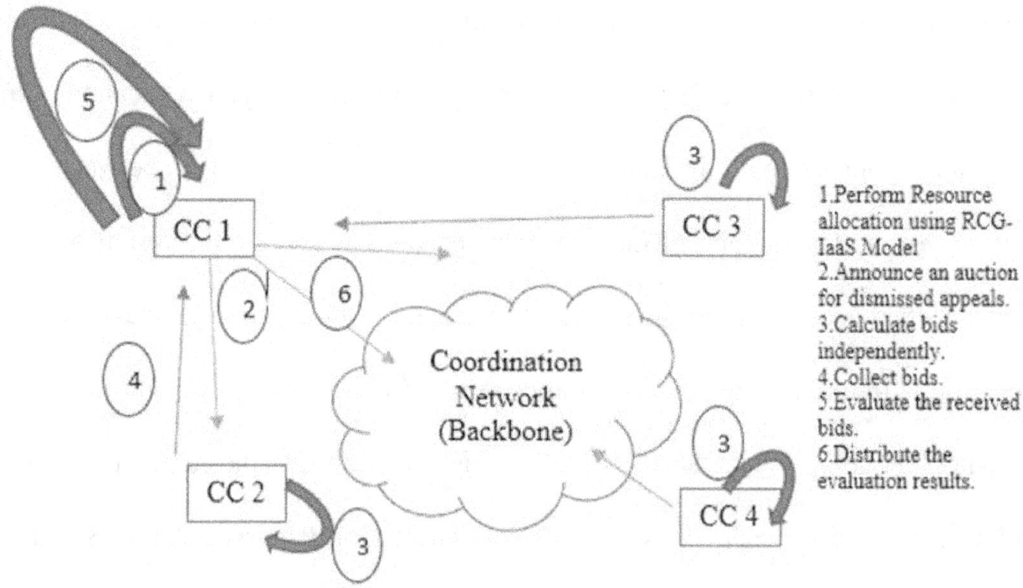

4.2(a) Transmitter Outlook

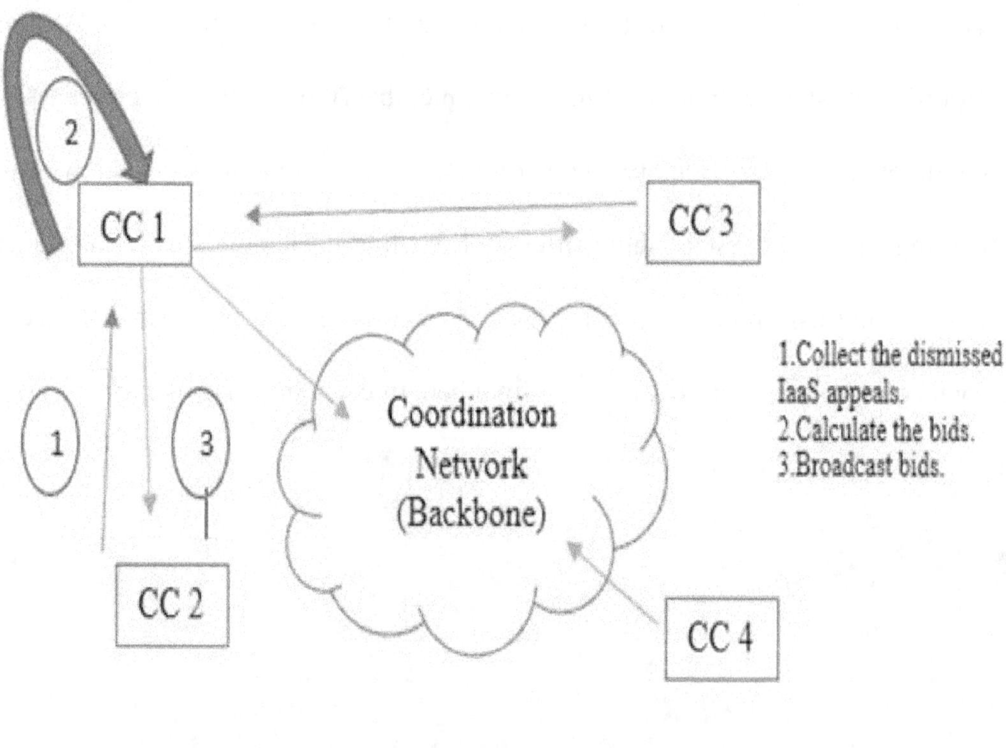

4.2 (b) Recipient Outlook

Figure 4.2: Steps of CC 1 operations communicate the project's outcomes to the deal's participants.

4. Perform a second cycle of territorial asset distribution by receiving regional resource allocation models based on solicitations provided by various clusters as a consequence of bartering.

5. Integrate the Cloud Service Provider advantage into each cluster.

The closeout mechanism progresses from the first to the following cycle by receiving a single offer fixed value sell-off component from Cluster Coordinators. This method achieves the optimal level coordination. Additionally, it is worth noting that Cloud Service Provider benefit is achieved by aggregating the calculated benefit in each focus. Correspondence between different Cluster Coordinators is facilitated by defining a common cluster as a result of each Cluster Coordinator having a one-of-a-kind identification. Systematization of the two assignments is critical for increasing the effectiveness of resource designation, particularly in large-scale conditions (C. Lee, 2015). To accomplish this efficiently, a vertical coordination has been accomplished by utilizing a two-tiered side sale component between the two progressive levels. The suggested method then repeats the first cycle, during which each Cluster Coordinator collects the IaaS requests received in its location (stage-1). After that, each location is free to manage the assets associated with the collected solicitations by using the RCG-IaaS model and calculating its profit (stage-2). Following the completion of the first cycle of asset allocation, each Cluster Coordinator checks for dismissed demands and reports a closeout if any exist by completing assignment (1) (step-3-a). During the interval, each Cluster Coordinator inspects for other members' declarations (that is, Cluster Coordinators) in mutual zone and responds to them by per-shaping assignment (2). (Step-3-b). At that time, Cluster Coordinator starts communicating to other members the outcomes of either assignment (1) or assignment (2). These assignment outcomes are referred to as the evaluation outputs for both accepting offers and establishing offers for existing declarations as a consequence of assignment (1) and assignment (2). (Step-3-c). At that point, the approach advances to the second focus on resource identification and final benefit calculations (stages-4 & 5).

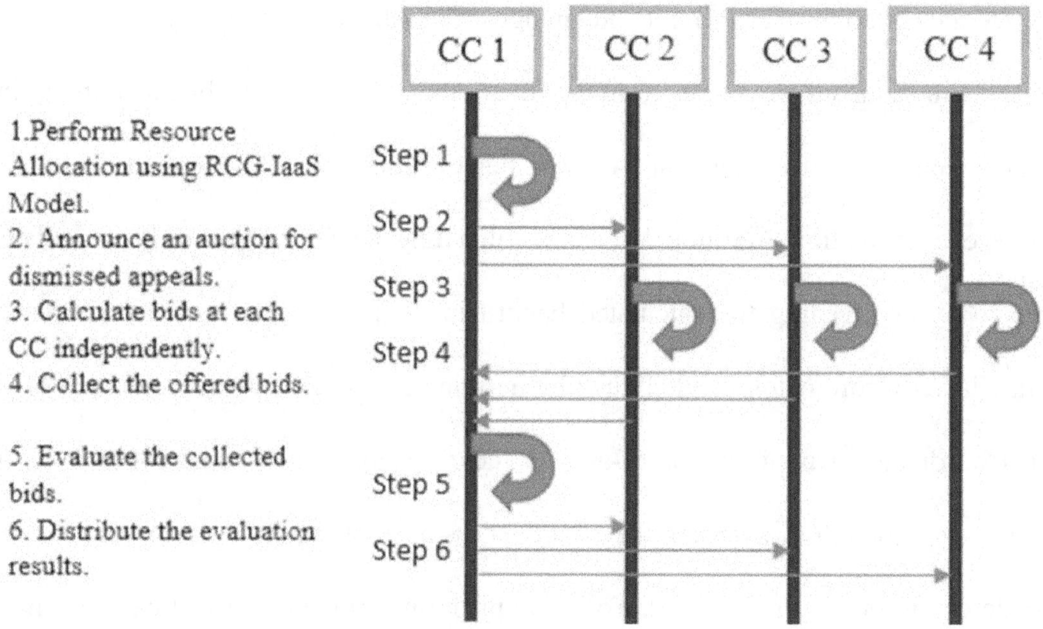

Figure 4.3: Succession of the operational-steps execution

Method Algo. 1 Assignment 1: Declare Vendue

1: Data In: Bunch of N Dismissed IaaS Appeal I_n = ($NRes_n$, $NCon_n$, Bid_n)

2: Data Out: Declaration of Dismissed In to G Cluster_Coordinators, $Assign_{n,g}$

3: Declare Vendue through setting dismissed appeals (appeals) in a split available cluster.

4: Assemble arriving offers through every cluster in $Bid_{n,g}$.

5: Integrate arriving offers into 1 record $AllBid_{n,g} \leftarrow Bid_{n,g}$.

6: Classify $AllBid_{n,g}$ in decreasing manner.

7: for each (I_n) in (N) do

8: if $I_n = AllBid_{n,g}$ and $AllBid_{n,g} > 0$ then

Place $Assign_{n,g}$=1

continue

end if

end for

Broadcast $Assign_{n,g}$ to every vanquishing clusters.

Method Algo. 2 Assignment 2: Link declared Vendue (Auction)

Data In: Bunch of N Dismissed IaaSappeal $I_n = (NRes_n, NCon_n, Bid_n)$

Data Out: Bid Record $OFFER\_List_g$

while true do

Assemble the declared dismissed appeals on a REJ_List_g.

Classify REJ_List_g in decreasing manner.

if size ($REJ\_ List_g$) ≥ 0 then

for each (I_n) in $REJ\_ List_g$ do

if $(C^g_v - NRes_n \geq 0)$ and $(B^g_{agg} - NCon_n \geq 0)$ then

$C^g{}_v \leftarrow C^g{}_v - NRes_n$

$B^g{}_a \leftarrow B^g{}_a - NCon_n$

Calculate Bid_n

$OFFER\_ List_g = Bid_n$

else

$OFFER\_List_g = 0$

end if

end for

end if

18: Broadcast $OFFER\_List_g$ to other participants

19: end while

Currently, Cluster Coordinator has declared a closeout on a shared open area and is waiting for offers from other members (line-three). Cluster Coordinators begin gathering offers from other members (line four), and then consolidate the collected offers into a single rundown $AllBid_{n,g}$ (line five). Each Cluster Coordinator begins by sorting and assessing the aggregated bids submitted in response to each solicitation included in the sliding request (line six). It selects the most advantageous offer for each solicitation with the ultimate aim of increasing the CSPs overall profit. Meanwhile, proposals with no characteristics are rejected (lines seven-twelve). If the solicitation's associated offer an incentive in $Assign_{n,g}$ 0 or does not exist at the time of the computation, the calculation proceeds to the subsequent solicitation. Finally, each Cluster Coordinator initiates the process of advancing solicitations to the winning bid clusters (line thirteen).

The following assignment, indicated by calculation five, is a perplexing execution errand that monitors shared areas for any documented closeouts (line three). Each month, the Cluster Coordinator produces a REJ $List_g$ of all solicitations that have been deemed refused in the common area (line four). Then, it filters the rejected overview in sliding proposal according to the specific offers provided (line five). Additionally, the Cluster Coordinator analyses the availability of resources with each request and, if it has adequate assets, provides a fresh offer in response to the need; otherwise, it makes no offer (lines seven-sixteen). The new OFFER Listg lacks this assessment capability. OFFER Listg is reorganized into districts by the Cluster Coordinator. Finally, it sends to each region its comparative section in its offer list (line eighteen). After successfully completing the two tasks, each Cluster Coordinator receives additional requirements. At that time, the second cycle of asset designation begins, during which each Cluster Coordinator freely applies the asset distribution model (RCG-IaaS) to the solicitations received.

At the moment, the closeout process achieves the optimal level coordination. The advantages gained from such calculation may be diminished by selecting the highest acknowledgement percentage with the shortest distribution time. Despite the fact that this approach increased benefit, it did so at the expense of portion pricing. Additionally, it reduces the time required to assemble comparative dissemination computations, since the technique uses just two emphases. The assignment's trustworthiness is ensured by a bartering process that prevents duplication and declares a single champion.

The "Vickrey-Clarke-Groves" (VCG) component serves as a major benchmark for combinatorial sales, or more precisely, barters in which many items are offered concurrently and rivals may make offers on bundles of items. With the expectation of moveable benefit, the VCG component is essentially an intriguing system that achieves successful outcomes in commonly used processes in readily connected regions. The VCG method charges each chief their externality, thus obfuscating the leader's effect on others. Assume, however, that despite the presence of different criteria, a chief might join the closeout. For example, if the closeout is performed online, a bidder may use several usernames, and the dealer may not be able to verify that unique usernames correspond to distinct identities. On the other side, a leader may educate a select bidder to make an offer in their favour. At the moment, bidder is no longer a chief. The system will never be able to identify the leader again, and therefore will be unable to charge them with the externality they impose. The practise of using several characters, referred to as shill offering, may benefit a customer. (Y. Sakurai, 1999)

Shill sale (bidding) should be conducted fairly. Assume, for example, that two players exist, one of whom may use shills and is aware of the other's value. The value of participant 1 is very super modular, implying that the item is a complement to participant 1. Assume that participant 2 does two tasks proficiently. At that moment, in undominated processes in which participant 1 proposes honestly and participant 2 succeeds in at least two ways, a Nash equilibrium emerges (not really the bundle it would be productive for them to win). Participant 2 patronises one hawker for each item she wins. A seller of a particular commodity submits a bid for that item. Player 2 obtains a much better result than she would have had had she made an honest offer. As a consequence, since both parties have precisely super modular values and both win at least two things at the competent designation, the VCG process generates a large number of equilibria in undominated processes that are not outcome equal. This is in striking contrast to the VCG process, which demonstrates an unparalleled unity in undominated methods when shills are excluded.

Shill bidding is intrinsically linked to intrigue. Leaving aside the conventional motivation to suppress competition, the disincentive to collapse by using shills when confronted with a similar value transform into a motivator to converge for an alliance when confronted with a similar valuation. When estimates are included, compelling motivations to sell and consolidate may disappear.

The VCG approach is basically a single competent selling method based on straightforward offering (Green, J., 1977), (HolmstRom. B., 1979). By essentially unique, 'I' means that with each bidder 'I', the instalments may be adjusted on a regular basis in accordance with the bidders' records. Due to a number of disadvantages (Milgrom, 2004), (Ausubel& Milgrom, 2006), and (Rothkopf, M., 2007), the VCG method cannot be utilized to sell a diverse range of heterogeneous articles. The reason for examining this process is because it is a one-of-a-kind closeout followed by a range of enticing goods, and we want to determine if these possessions really help with certain issues.

4.3 Simulation Scenarios and Experimental Analysis

Now draw conclusions on examination of shill offering. The consequence of this area is that there is often an incentive for a prospective bidder to employ shills or for a potential bidder partnership to consolidate.

To refine the inquiry, it is beneficial to eliminate the competition effect–which exists even in a closeout for a single item. The link between the urge to split into distinct characters and the incentive for multiple personalities to combine has been studied in a variety of contexts, for example, split- and consolidate-proofness in planning issues.

A motivation for forming an alliance and the urge to push transforms into a deterrent for forming an alliance. Both of these driving factors disappear simultaneously when additional material values are considered. It is necessary to bear in mind that there is some imbalance between peddler offering and combining in that, unlike peddler offering, combining does not result in unnecessary classifications among bidders; nevertheless, blending reduces the vender's income. We conclude the segment by noting that the problem of perfect conspiracy has much the same structure as the issue of optimal peddler providing at the moment (expecting the alliance can reallocate the merchandise after the closeout). If there are the same number of alliance members as goods for sale, this additional criterion cannot be met, and optimal plot degrades to ideal peddler offering.

As we have chosen the problem statement of addressing collusion in a cluster-distributed resource-allocation method as our starting point (Khaled Metwally, 2018). We used the IBM

CPLEX LOG simulation (IBM ILOG CPLEX Optimizer, 2015) to show that if a bidding process occurs, the objective is to find the least expensive assignment of without complicity, assigning bids to bidders. The studies were carried out on a Hewlett-Packard computer equipped with a 2.3 GHz Intel-Core -5 processor and 8 GB of random-access memory running Windows 10 home single language and using the IBM CPLEX solver with C++ programming. A few bidders are attempting to get a massive deal. The contract is divided into many duties. Certain jobs are critical and must be awarded to the highest bidder. Others are not critical, and if they remain unassigned, a liability is imposed. Each bidder may make an offer for a subset of the undertakings, and each assignment may be optional or mandatory in the bid. While a discretionary assignment offer may be accepted separately, mandatory assignment offers are win or lose: mandatory assignments must be accepted in their whole or all will be rejected for each offer. The aim is to award the lowest-priced job to bidders.

The following is a description of the Data File in which TaskSet describes the bid, task, cost, and an option:

TaskSet = (<b1, t1, 123, 0>, <b1, t2, 110, 0>, <b1, t3, 123, 1>, <b1, t5, 123, 1>, <b2, t2, 123, 0>, <b2, t3, 100, 0>, <b2, t4, 123, 0>, <b2, t5, 123, 1>, <b3, t1, 100, 1>)

Tasks are described as follows:

Tasks= (t1, t2, t3, t4, t5)

Task penalty described below with task and cost as follows:

Task Penalty= If cost is -1 it means it must be assigned.

<task =t1 and cost=120>

<task =t2 and cost=120>

<task =t3 and cost=minus1>

<task =t4 and cost=120>

<task =t5 and cost=120>

Method Algorithm for cheapest assignment to the competitors (bidders) perspective.

1. Data In: convention data structures follow: tuple task = (bid, task, price, option)

Tuple bid= (bid, task) and tuple penalty = (task, cost)

Basic data: Bids for tasks, all tasks, Penalty for unassigned tasks. If cost is -1, it means, it must be assigned.

2. Data Out: Cheapest Assignment to the bidders

3. conclude sets: Set of <bids, task> pairs; If task ="REQD", it states that all tasks are compulsory for the bid; if task=A task name, it states that the task is optional.

Bids = {<t.bid, "REQD"> | t in Task Set: t.option == 0} union {<t.bid, t.task> | t in Task Set : t.option == 1}

Set of all bids including task u; "REQD" indicates u is compulsory for the bid

Bid Tasks [u in Tasks] = {<t.bid, "REQD"> | t in Task Set: t.option == 0 &&t. task == u} union

{<t.bid, t.task> | t in Task Set : t.option == 1 &&t.task == u}

4. conclude data: float Bid Cost[<b,t> in Bids] =sum (<b,t,price,opt> in Task Set) price +sum (<b,t2,price,opt> in Tas kSet : t == "REQD" && opt == 0) price

assert sum (b in Bids) BidCost[b] >= 0

MaxBidCost = max (b in Bids) BidCost[b]

float Penalty [Tasks] = [t.task: (t.cost==-1) ? 1+MaxBidCost: t.cost | t in TaskPenalty]

5. Variables for decision: dvarboolean Awards [Bids], 1 when awarded; 0 otherwise dvarboolean Avoid [tasks], 1 if not allocated to the job; 0 if not assigned;

6. Objective value = cost of accepted bids + penalty for unassigned tasks

dexpr float AcceptedBidsCost = sum (b in Bids) Bid Cost[b]*Award[b]

dexpr float Unassigned Task Penalty Cost = sum (t in Tasks) Penalty[t]*Avoid[t]

7. Mode l: minimize Accepted Bids Cost +Unassigned Task PenaltyCost

Subject to Assignment constraint: each task must be assigned to a bid

For all (t in Tasks)

ct Assign: sum (b in Bid Tasks[t]) Award[b] == 1 - Avoid[t]

tuple Award Solution T= (Bids, value)

Award Solution = {<i0, Award [i0]> | i0 in Bids

tuple Avoid Solution T= (Tasks, value)

Avoid Solution = <i0, Avoid[i0]> | i0 in Tasks

8. Post-processing: bid Awarded = <t.bid, t.task> | t in Task Set :(t.option == 0 && Award[<t.bid, "REQD">] == 1) || (t.option == 1 && Award[<t.bid, t.task>] == 1)

Avoided = {t | t in Tasks: Avoid[t] == 1

Total Avoided = sum (t in Tasks) Avoid[t]

execute display: (Award, Awarded, Avoided, Total Avoided)

for (var b in Bids)

Bid Cost[b]

End for

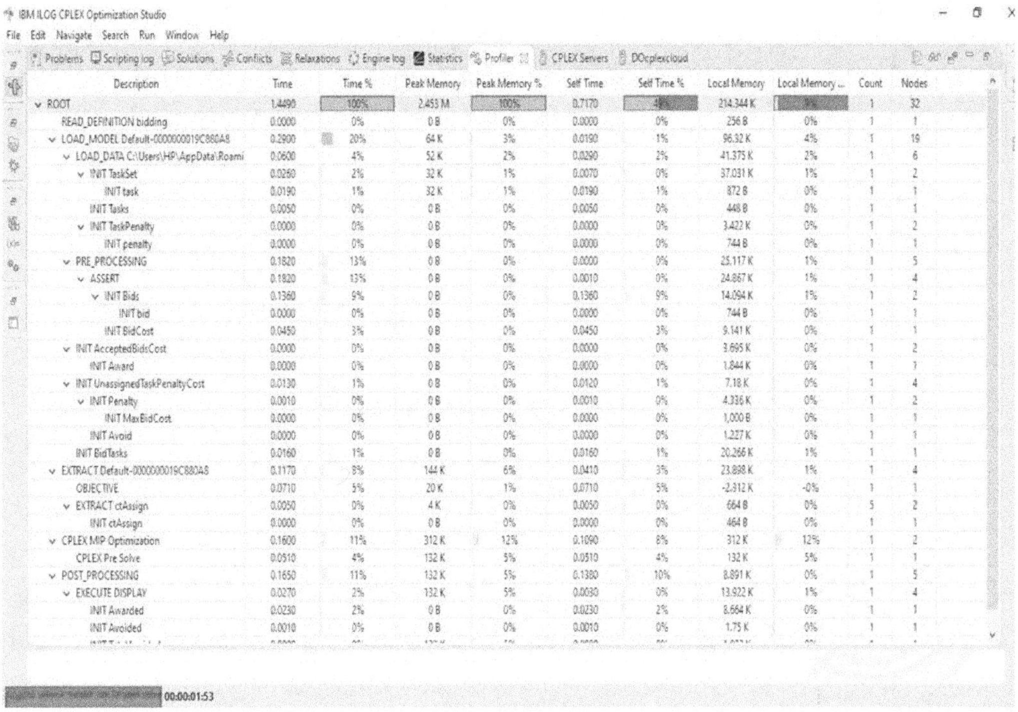

(a) **Profiler: Peak Time of cheapest assignment**

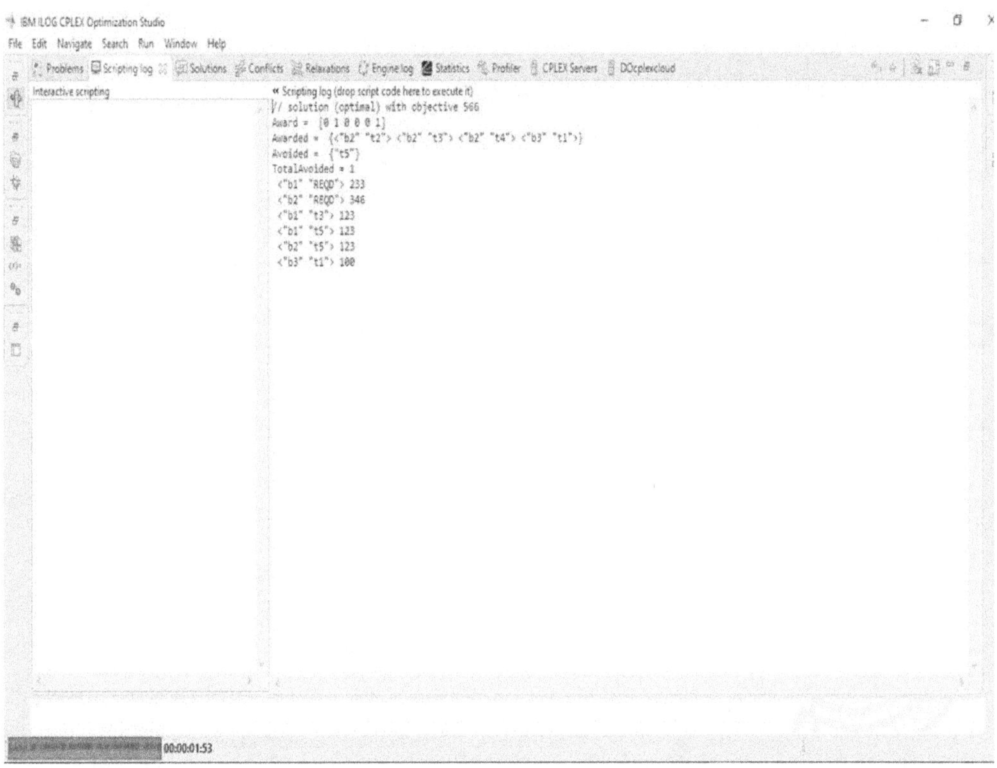

(b) **Scripting Log: Award and avoid data**

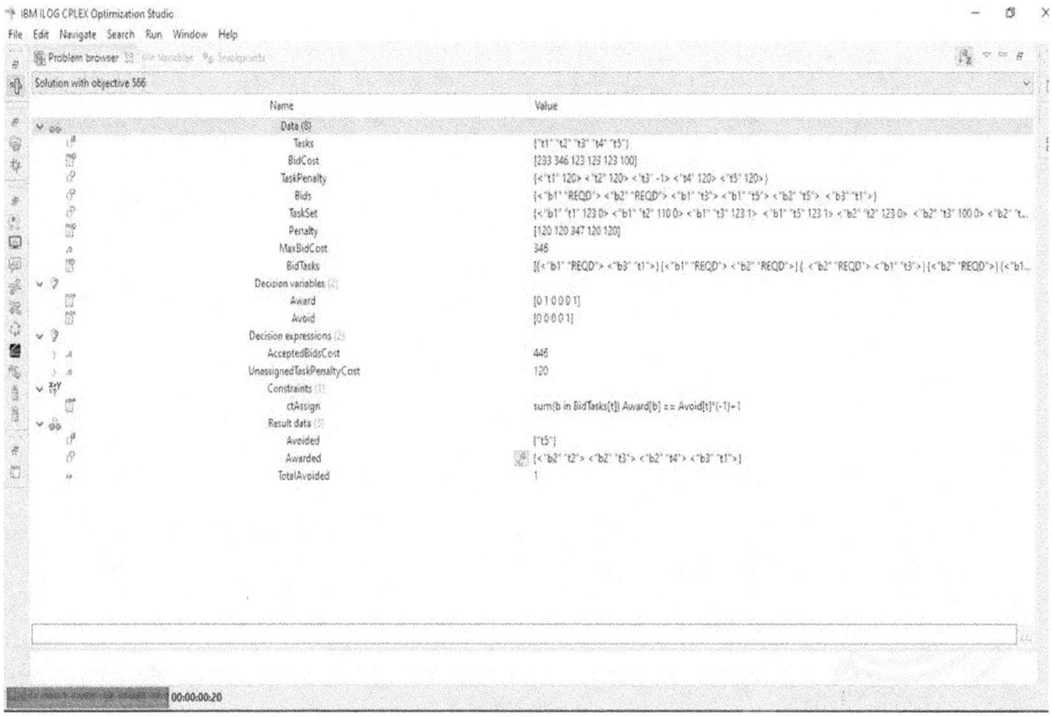

(c) Bidding Solution with result data

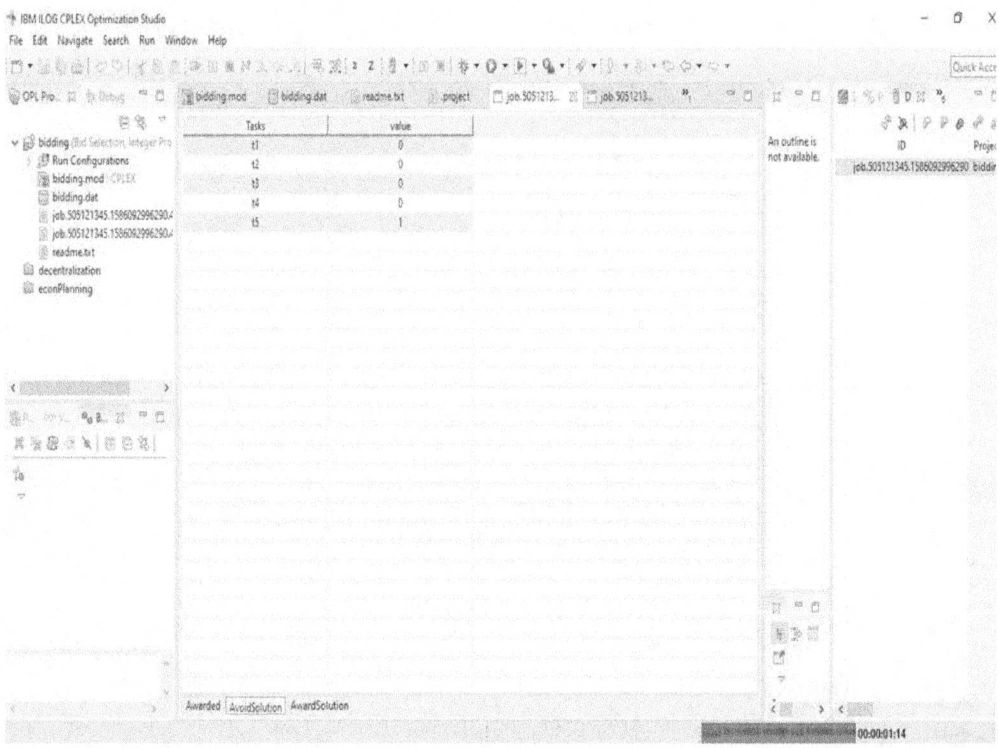

(d) Avoid Solution

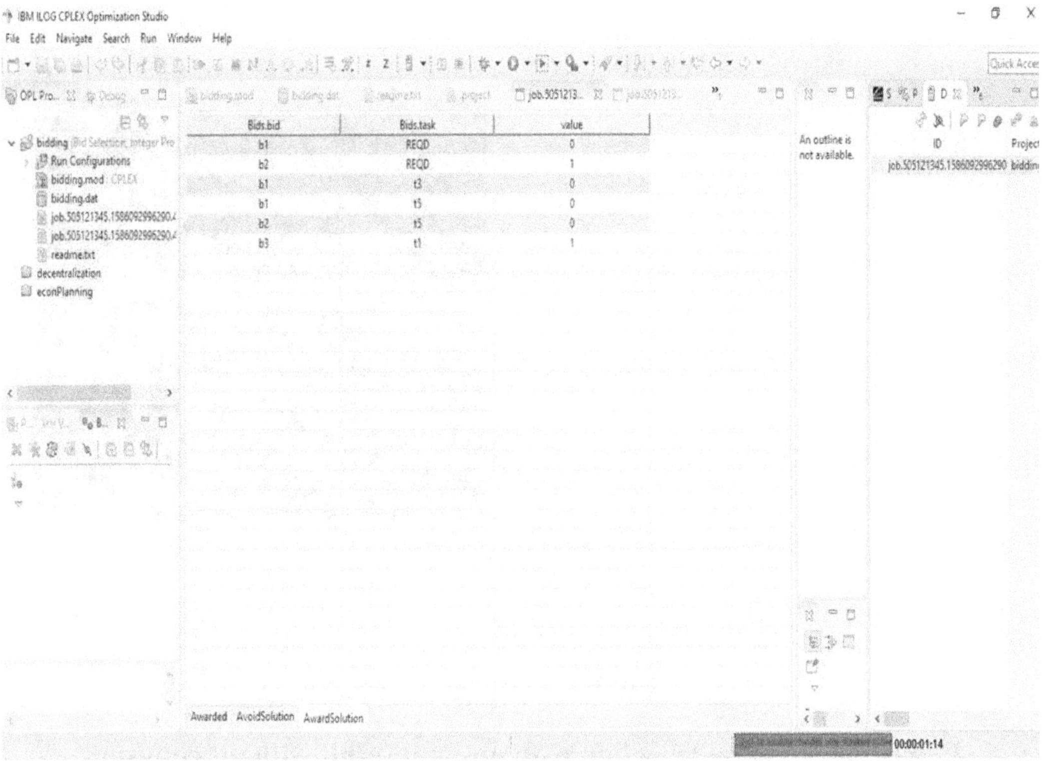

(e) Award Solution

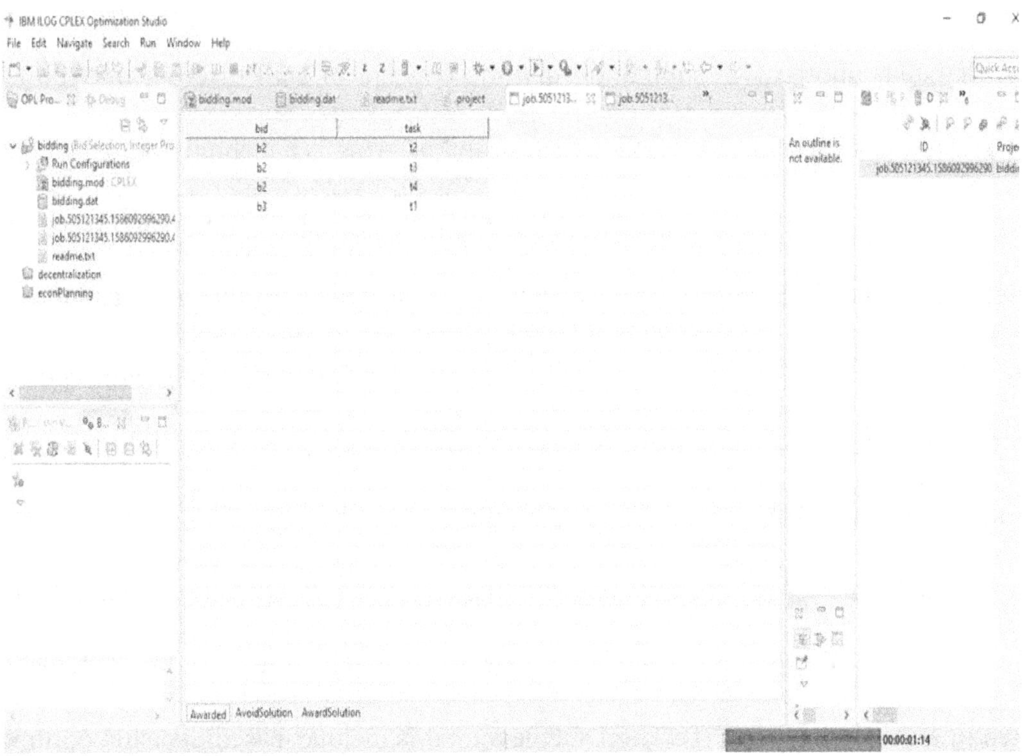

(f) Awarded Bid

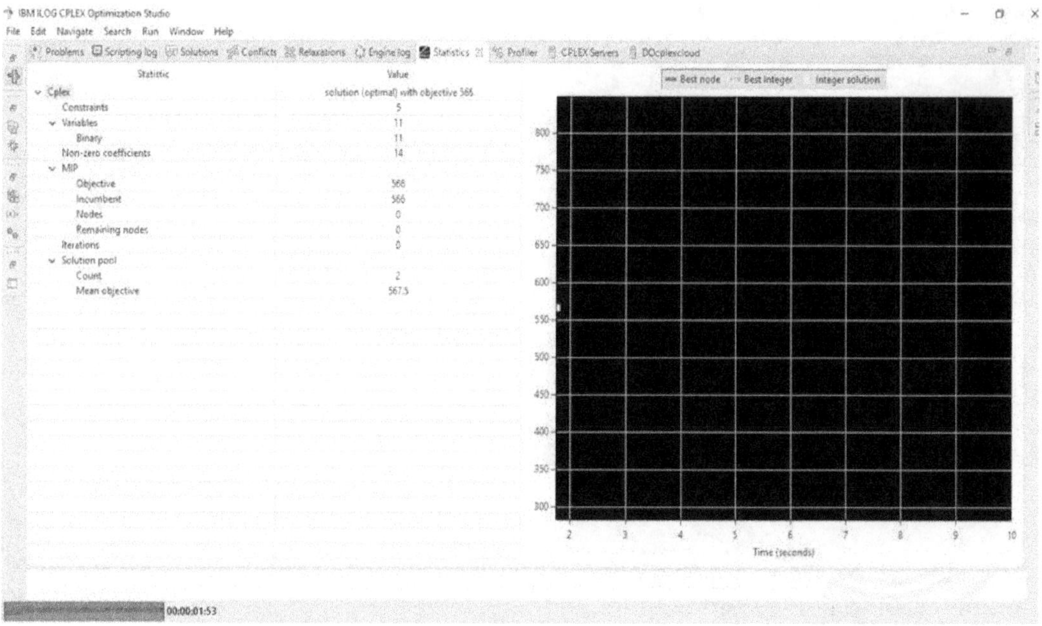

(g) Bidding Statistics with plot

Figure 4.4: Bidding Selection with optimal result without collusion

4.4 Summary

Finally, the study showed via simulation that the concept of shill offering may be used to combinatorial sell-offs using the VCG method. Shill offering is a technique in which a single leader participates in bartering under a variety of guises. Using this approach, research used Task Set, Tasks, and Task Penalty (if the cost is -1, the task must be allocated) as inputs to the system and determined the most cost-effective way of allocating assignments to bidders, as shown in Figure 4.4. (g). The figures 4.4 (a) and (b) depict the Peak Time for the cheapest assignment and award & avoid data, respectively, in the form of scripting logs. On Docplexcloud, Figure 4.4 (c) illustrates the bidding solution with outcome data and Figure 4.4 (d) illustrates the avoid solution. The award solution, which avoided a bid on Docplexcloud, is shown in Figure 4.4 (e) and (f). The DOcplexcloud is a cloud-based decision optimization system that solves optimization issues. This demonstrates that after the assignment restriction is applied, each job must be allocated to a bid, and then the optimum solution is determined by the cheapest assignment of tasks to bidders without collusion.

Chapter 5: 5. 1 Introduction

IaaS provisioning is one of the most exciting aspects of cloud computing applications since it enables the deployment of different applications. IaaS is a cloud computing model that enables the supply of mission-critical computing infrastructure for the deployment of business applications via the Internet. This includes components such as storage, hardware, servers, and networking. IaaS often relocates the physical architecture of IT applications offshore and a service provider gives customers access to a virtualized environment with processing services. The efficient execution of each Infrastructure-as-a-Service provisioning system (Metwally, 2015) allows the basic CG model to be extended and modified to function on a cluster scale across many backbone-connected data centres. Extra Data Center bandwidth (Intra/Inter) constraints and variable regional prices are handled in this extended architecture. The objective varies by range: in the private cloud process, the primary objective is to decrease IT services' Capital Expenditures (CAPEX) and Operating Expenditures (OPEX). The public cloud model is geared at optimizing CSP net profit (Breitgand and Glikson, 2013). The fundamental function of CG technology is its decomposition approach for resolving resource distribution issues: infrastructure-as-a-Service provisioning is decomposed into a key problem and a valuation problem (M. E. Ubbecke & J. Desrosiers, 2005). Additionally, CG operates with a minimal number of columns, resulting in the primary issue with the restriction. (RPI) restricted primary issue ensured that CG would control numerous variables and constraints in a streamlined manner. As the price is reduced significantly, the pricing problem is addressed iteratively and the appropriate part of the RPI is appended. Otherwise, the most recent cure is flawless. A column represents the actual assignment of VRs to IaaS. The primary issue and valuation problem are connected by transferring the component duties of the key issue variables to the price problem. In our distributed design, each cluster contains Data Centers that form the pooled pool of Vg.

The proposed proposal is for one cluster. Whereas Cdq and Ad show the capacity of QoS q, Q, and comprehensive intra-bandwidth in Data Center d, respectively, with n/w, Bl shows the remaining BW on n/w link l, where L represents a collection of connections connecting the whole cluster of Data Centers. The following is the definition of the CG formulation (RCG-IaaS). We recast the IaaS capital sharing conundrum for Individual Infrastructure Allocating Configurations (IIACs), where each IaaS request allocation configuration is specified by a c-indexed IIAC. An IIAC may be used to express IIACc = (Vc; Pc), where Vc is a collection of VRs and Pc is a collection of routes used to satisfy user needs. A chain of connections comprised of each route Pc, where Vc; Lc, Vg. In this approach, customers may define IaaS requests as in = (Vn; Kn; Pn), where Vn is a list of requested VRs, Kn is a collection of bandwidth-bn connections between the VRS, and Pn is the customer's willing to pay offer. The decision variable c is defined as follows: it equals 1 if the IIAC c is utilised in the IaaS provisioning solution, and 0 otherwise. By accepting more IaaS requests and lowering setup costs, we aim to boost CSP sales.

A novel optical backbone virtualization method for inter-data centre networks. Because the inter-DC n/w must be activated again to provide time-of-use awareness for cloud device traffic, the authors propose a virtual annealing heuristic. (2017) (B. Kantarci & H. Mouftah)

Numerous approaches have been suggested to address IaaS's fundamental issues, including scalability and numerical complexity. Both have an effect on the correctness of the answer. The majority of proposals (A. Ahmed, 2013), (S. Zhang, 2014), (I. Houidi, 2008), (F. Samuel, 2013), (B. Kantarci & H. Mouftah, 2017), (Q. Zhang, 2012), and (M. Alicherry & T.

Lakshman, 2012) emphasize a two-step centralized provisioning approach, with the first phase mapping virtual nodes and the second phase signing virtual routing links. All incoming requests are collected by a single hub. The following is a centralized, sequential approach.

Provisioning nodes and connections in two phases results in reduced energy consumption and a greater number of rejected requests, which reduces the cost of CSP.

The non-scalable heuristic method accelerates response times, resulting in suboptimal IaaS supply and quality of service.

Algorithm for multi-agent routing using heuristics. Each node was given a mapping algorithm using this approach. They did, however, conduct a small-scale study to determine the plan's effectiveness and scalability. Scaling the method to thousands of substratum nodes resulted in performance degradation (I. Houidi, 2008).

The PolyViNE, which organizes the process of VN embedding with the relevant infrastructure suppliers (InPs). Prior to forwarding embedded nodes, an InP develops its own local resource allocation system and links to a nearby InP. The procedure was repeated until the whole request was encapsulated. The authors of PolyViNE identified many issues: scalability, response time, and overhead computation. All of these problems can be resolved more simply in a decentralized system. (Samuel, F., 2013)

A unified method that utilises an ILP and max-cut flow algorithm to split IaaS requests from different InPs. Their strategy relies on a centralized approach, which raises concerns about scalability. Breaking IaaS requests often results in inefficiencies that are unacceptable for a large number of modern apps. (I. Houidi, 2011)

5.2 Principal Issue and Problem

The issue of IaaS provisioning may be stated using the vectors c, cC. The IaaS provisioning problem then chooses the full N settings. The design is optimal for accommodating all requirements, and each authorization is granted by its IIAC. It is compatible with the so-called main query for selecting the appropriate IIAC settings. COSTc denotes the cost of an IIAC c, taking into account all VRs and configuration routes. REVc is defined as the advantage of utilising an IIAC c to fulfil a series of N IaaS requirements.

$$REV_c = \sum_{n \in N} a^c_n P_n - COST_c \quad (1)$$

Where:

a^c_n represents that $IIAC_c$ set-out Infrastructure-as-a-Service appeal n.

P_n means, the present bid by appeal n.

Configuration costs are measured below:

$$COST_c = \sum_{v \in V_c} \zeta^c_{v}.c_v + \sum_{l \in L_c} b_l.c^b_l + \sum_{l \in L_c} \gamma^c_{b}.\, c^i_l \quad (2)$$

where:

ζ^c_v - variable shows the configuration c uses VR v.

γ^c_b - configuration c deploy Intra-bandwidth b.

b_l- in configuration c deploy n/w link 1 for inter-Data Center bandwidth

c_v, c^b_l, and c^i_l - in configuration c, these are just the prices associated with virtual reality, inter- and intra-data center connectivity.

Principal issue and problem, denoted by Principal-IAP, & is described below:

Target Task:

$$\text{Greatest.} \sum_{c \in C} REV_c \lambda_c \quad (3)$$

Constraints:

$\sum \sum \zeta^c_v.\lambda_c \leq C^d_{q}, \forall\ q\epsilon Q, \forall\ d\epsilon D$ $\quad(\delta^d_q)$ (4)

$c\epsilon C\ v\epsilon V_q$

$\sum \gamma^c_b.\lambda_c \leq A_d, \forall\ d\epsilon D$ $\quad(\phi_d)$ (5)

$c\epsilon C$

$\sum \lambda_{c}.b_l \leq B_l, \forall\ l\epsilon L$ $\quad(\eta_l)$ (6)

$c\epsilon C$

$\sum \lambda c.a^c{}_n \leq 1, \forall\ n\epsilon N$ $\quad(\alpha_n)$ (7)

$c\epsilon C$

$\sum \lambda c \leq N$ $\quad(\beta)$ (8)

$c\epsilon C$

$\lambda c\ \epsilon\ \{0, 1\}$ (9)

Equations (four, five, and six) imply that the VRs, intra/inter-BW, that were previously employed have been eliminated. Equations (four, five, and six) imply that the VRs, intra/inter-BW, that were previously employed have been eliminated. Equation (seven) demonstrates that for each authorised IaaS order, a maximum of one IIAC may be selected. Equation (Eight) eventually improves the likelihood that IIAC can be selected to meet all N IaaS requirements. Equation (Nine) concentrates on the main variable integral.

Pricing dilemma

The valuation issue generates an extra IIAC setup. As stated before, one new column is added to the RPI at a little reduced price as a consequence of repeatedly answering the pricing question. It is detailed below. Assume that (dq), (d), (l), (n), and () are dual variables aligned with constraints (four), (five), (six), and (seven) in the main issue (eight). As such, it is also acceptable to define the cost savings as follows:

$$BAR(REV_c) = REV_c - \sum_{n \epsilon N} \alpha_n . a^c_n - \sum_{l \epsilon L} \eta_l . b_l - \sum_{d \epsilon D} \sum_{q \epsilon Q} \delta^d_q - \sum_{d \epsilon D} \phi_d . \gamma^c_b - \beta \quad (10)$$

To describe the reduced cost equation in price variables, we specify the following decision variables:

z_n: Indicates whether or not an IaaS request n is granted by configuration c ε C.

x^v_r: Indicates if a requested resource r has been assigned to a virtual resource v.

y^p_k: It indicates whether or not a relation k uses path p.

We extract correlations b/w price problem parameters & principal problem coefficient:

∀ c ϵ C & n ϵ N, now:

$$a^c_n = z_n \quad (11)$$

∀ link l ϵ L, now:

$$b_l = \sum_{n \epsilon N} \sum_{k \epsilon K_n} \sum_{p \epsilon P_c} \sum_{n \epsilon N} \Pi^p_l . b_n . y^p_k \quad (12)$$

Where: Π^p_l -variable shows, In path p, the relation l is used. ∀ c ϵ C & asset v ϵ V_c, now:

$$\zeta^c_v = \sum \sum x^v_r \quad (13)$$

∀ intra Data Center bandwidth b, now:

$$\gamma^c_b = \sum_{n \epsilon N} \sum_{k \epsilon K_n} \sum_{p \epsilon P_c} \sum_{n \epsilon N} \Pi^p_l . b_n . y^p_k \quad (14)$$

Intra-Data Center routes, though, believed to be single-hop paths, i.e. $\sum_{l \epsilon L p} \Pi^p_l = 1$ As an oversubscription element being used data centre networking networks, the allotted bandwidth for multiple links in each direction was indirectly shielded. Equ. (fourteen) as smooth as written below:

$$\gamma^{c}{}_{b} = \sum_{n\epsilon N} \sum_{k\epsilon K_n} \sum_{p\epsilon P_c} b_{n}.y^{p}{}_{k} \quad (15)$$

Consequently, the principal issue and problem target task (Equ.10) and constraint described below.

Target:

$$BAR\,(REV_c) = \sum_{n\epsilon N} z_n.P_n - COST_c - \sum_{n\epsilon N} \alpha_n.z_n - \sum_{l\epsilon L} \eta_l X \sum_{n\epsilon N} \sum_{k\epsilon K_n} \sum_{p\epsilon P_c} \sum_{l\epsilon l_p} \Pi^{p}{}_{l}.b_n.y^{p}{}_{k} - \sum_{d\epsilon D} \sum_{q\epsilon Q} \delta^{d}{}_{q} - \sum_{d\epsilon D} \phi_d.\,X \sum_{n\epsilon N} \sum_{k\epsilon K_n} \sum_{p\epsilon P_c} b_n.y^{p}{}_{k} - \beta \quad (16)$$

Where:

$$COST_c = \sum_{n\epsilon N} [\sum_{r\epsilon R_n} \sum_{v\epsilon V} x^{v}{}_{r}.c_v + \sum_{k\epsilon K_n} \sum_{p\epsilon P_c} \sum_{l\epsilon L_p} b_n.\,\Pi^{p}{}_{l}\,.y^{p}{}_{k}.c_l] \quad (17)$$

Constraints:

$$\sum_{v\epsilon V_q} x^{v}{}_{r} \leq z_n, \forall (\text{“}r \in R_n\text{”}, \forall \text{“}n \in N\text{”}, \forall \text{“}q \in Q\text{”}) \quad (18)$$

$$\sum_{p\epsilon P} y^{p}{}_{k} \leq z_n, \forall (\text{“}k \in K_n\text{”}, \forall \text{“}n \in N\text{”}) \quad (19)$$

$$x^{v}{}_{r}.x^{v'}{}_{r'} \geq y^{p}{}_{k}, \forall (\text{“}v, v' \in P\text{”}, \forall \text{“}r, r' \in K_n\text{”}), \quad (20)$$

$$L\,(p) \leq \epsilon, \forall\ p \in P_n \quad (21)$$

$$\sum z_n \leq 1 \quad (22)$$

Equ. (Eighteen) ensure just one VR for each resource needed. Equ. (Nineteen.'s and Twenty) means just one direction for each link. Equ. (Twenty-one) communicate QoS specifications for link allocation with a maximum number of hops. Equ. (Twenty-two) implies that each

IIAC produced can handle one IaaS order.

5.3 HCIA Model Solution

We are now debating ways to circumvent the HCIA model. To begin, the RPI must be setup with a collection of fake columns with zero income. For IAP questions, the top bounds are determined using a simple relaxation. The relaxation of the principal-IAP is accomplished by relaxing the constraint in Eq. (Nine) to c 2 [0;1]; c C. The measures to solution method are given by a dual nested loop procedure.

I) Configure RPI with zero-income dummy tables.

II) Solve Principal-LPR with CPLEX solver.

III) Solve the price dilemma using ideal dual variables.

IV) Fine-tune the price problem in order to identify a new column.

A) Whenever positive cost-reduced col^{m}. has been observed, link and re-optimize this segment with the principal-LPR. Otherwise, it is optimally solved by Principal-LPR.

B) We re-establish credibility constraints on λ to evaluate the principal-IAP integer solution and begin with CPLEX solver branch-and-bound. Notably, the conclusion of the principal-LPR solution means that the optimum upper limit for the principal-IAP solution has been reached. We must then have an integer solution to the IaaS provisioning issue in order to obtain an integer solution to Principal-IAP, reinstate the integrity limit, and address the principal-problem using a branch-and-bound method.

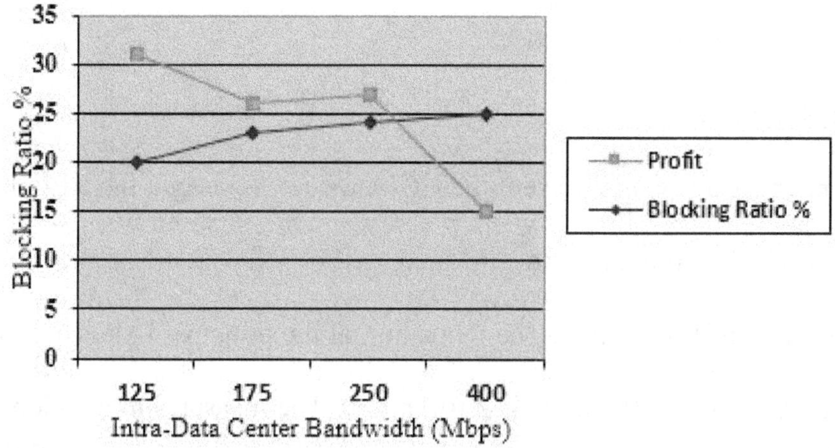

(a) Fifty-IaaS of Intra Bandwidth (Intra-Data Center Bandwidth (Mbps))

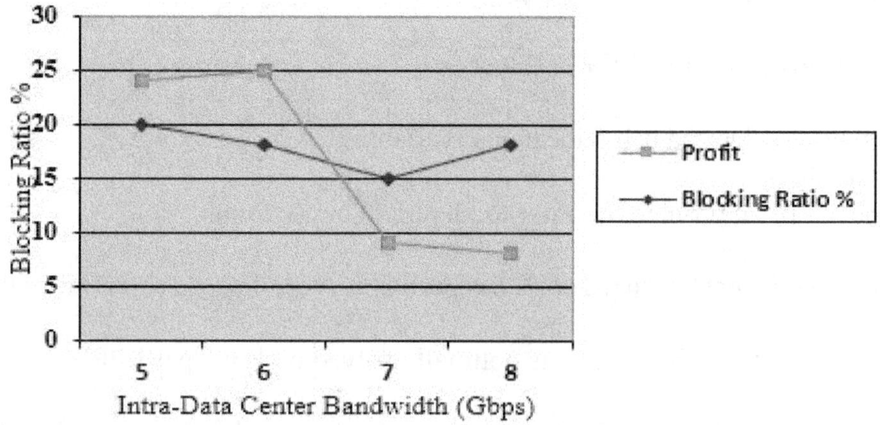

(b) Hundred-IaaS of Intra Bandwidth

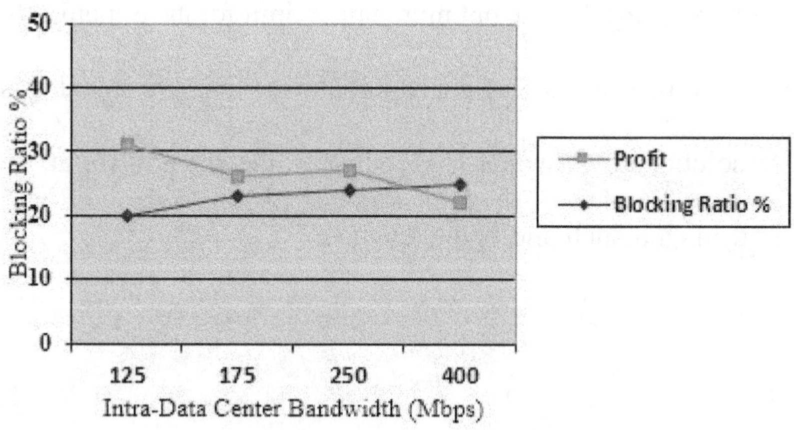

(c) Hundred-IaaS of Inter bandwidth

Figure 5.1: Inter/Intra-Data Center variations of Profit-Blocking trade-off

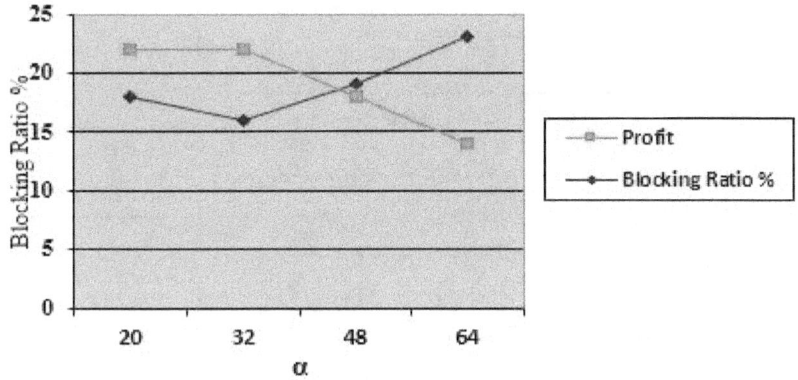

(a) α-ratio-one

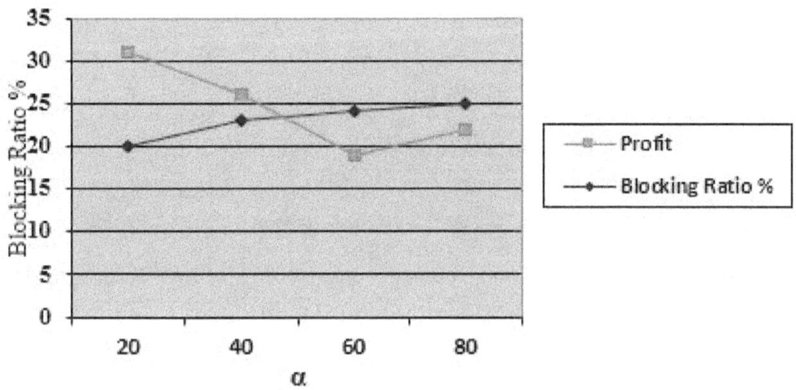

(b) α-ratio-two

Figure 5.2: Impact variations of BW (Inter/Intra Data-center)

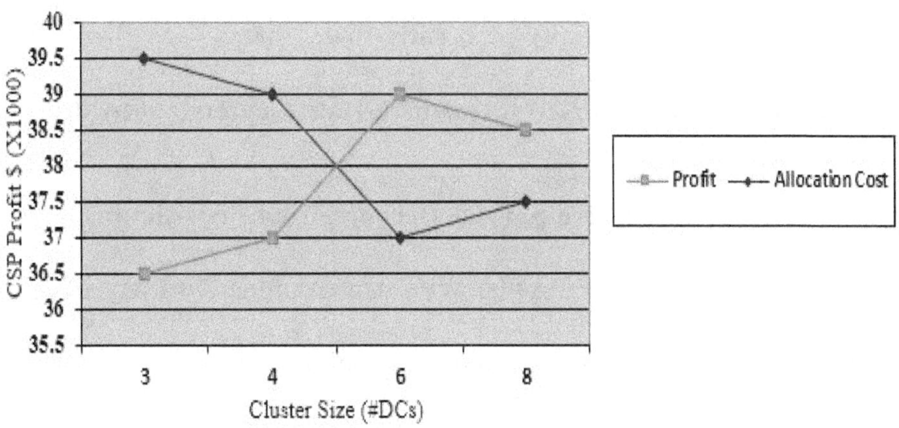

Figure 5.3: Differences in the cluster size, Profit-Cost trade-off

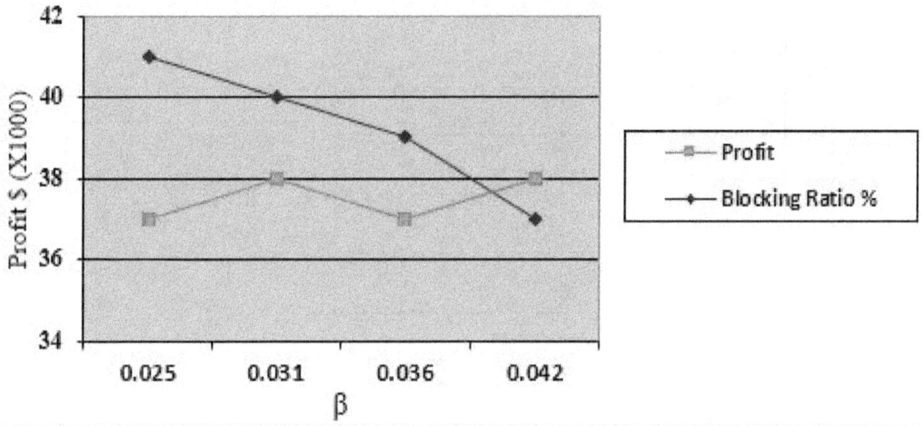

(a) β-ratio-one

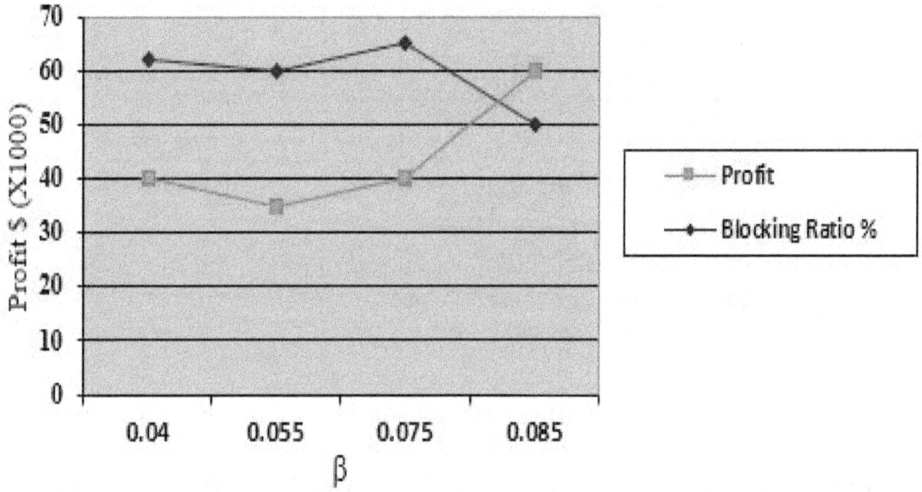

(a) β-ratio-two

Figure 5.4: Variations of Intra/Inter-Data Center Bandwidth.

5.4 Discourse of Infrastructure-as-a-Service Decentralized Provisioning

This section summarizes our study results. We often examine a variety of market pricing models and provide recommendations based on auctioning technique.

A. Dimensioning Distributed Structures:

This section covers the studies that have been conducted to determine the effectiveness and applicability of our suggested architecture in a particular programme. We investigate cluster granularity and the impact of data-center BW(Inter/Intra) changes. We focus on the asset instability associated with BW-as-a-cloud environment. Clearly, allocation in n/w-Inter-DC is too expensive. Intra-DC communication has an effect on customer loyalty, especially in latency-sensitive applications (Netflix). To begin, we conducted experiments to show the impact of variation on the blocking ratio and net benefit of variance, such as BW (Intra-Data-Center). The trade-off between Profit-Blocking Ratio and intra-data centre disparities is shown in Figures 1(a) and 1(b) for different workloads. The pooled bandwidth (Intra-) may be utilised to generate revenue for CSPs. BW) does not reach a server with a throughput of 250 Megabits per second (i.e., a four-to-one "oversubscription ratio").

When we examined the effect of the Inter-Data Center bandwidth gap, we found that our model performed well for a wide range of Infrastructure-as-a-Service requirements requiring bandwidth higher than 5 Gbps, as shown in Figure 5.1. (c). Costs rise drastically While we evaluated the effect of the Inter-Data Center bandwidth gap, we found that our model performed excellently even when serving a big group of Infrastructure-as-a-Service requests that required bandwidth higher than 5 Gbps, as shown in Figure 5.1. (c). Costs significantly decrease Furthermore, we discovered that when demand is low, the model prioritises data centre dispersion. This means that bandwidth variations across data centres have a negligible effect on our architecture. Our goal is to minimise CAPEX and OPEX expenses by optimizing inter/intra-data centre bandwidth use, reducing wasteful bandwidth utilisation, and preventing inefficient bandwidth utilisation. Utilizing bandwidth efficiently and avoiding This is done by defining and as the Inter/Intra and Intra/Inter ratios, respectively, and evaluating their effect on allocation costs and net profit (Equations (2) and (1)). Adjusting the blocking ratio and gain produces the results shown in Figures 5.2(a), 5.2(b), 5.4(a), and 5.4(b) (b). The purpose of defining is to optimize previously established bandwidth values, namely intra- and inter-data centre bandwidth. We found that the crossing point of the curve defining the gain breakpoint is different between = 42 and = 38 by comparing the data in Figures 5.2(a) and 5.2(b). These results corroborate our earlier observation that intra-data centre bandwidth ranged between 200 and 273 Mbps. The benefit threshold for Inter-Data Center bandwidth is between = 0.038 and = 0.076, which equates to 5.7 to 6.9 Gbps of Inter-Data Center bandwidth. This validated our prior design (Figure, more than 5 Gbps). 5.2.11 (c). To examine the cluster's potential granularity, Figure 4 illustrates the trade-off between CSPs' net profit (Eq. (1)) and the allocation cost (Eq. (2)) of the cluster's number of data centres. Beyond a cluster size of 5DCs, it can be shown that the suggested device maximised sales and reduced expenses during periods of heavy load. However, the pattern is inverted below that scale. The purpose of this thesis was to assist CSPs in developing a successful IaaS provisioning architecture. We focused on latency, which may cause network congestion and prevent CSPs from accepting more requests while they have sufficient capital. The numbers used in this study are variable and change according to template; nevertheless, as shown in (Gupta. Shashi Kant, 2020), they are consistent with our architectural scale. Additionally, other factors such as coverage area, demographics, renewable energy availability, and customer position preferences should be considered during design.

B. Pricing strategies for commercial cloud services; infrastructure-as-a-service Cloud-based service valuation model;

The major cloud providers (AWS, Azure, Google, and IBM) continue to reduce the cost of cloud resources. They provided discounts, expanded services, and, in some cases, reduced pricing increments to per-second charging. Costs decrease, but complexity increases. It is critical to understand how to navigate it. Cloud pricing varies according on the kind of services customers use, the clusters they choose, whether they utilise a local disc, and if they take advantage of promotional offers. Nonetheless, their pricing methods continue to be based on set price structures. The value criteria are uniform: the duration and quantity of services used, the location of cloud requests, the date of the transaction, the payment currency, and the kind of arrangement. Consider the following: Microsoft Azure Virtual Machine: Type A0: For US$0.020/hour, 1 virtual CPU, 0.75 GB RAM, and a 20 GB HDD are all accessible. It costs almost twice as much as the VM A1:1 Virtual Processor with 1.75 GB RAM and 70 GB HDD. On-demand services are a more successful valuation approach than being unable to obtain unexpected customer demand IaaS resources. It just considers the quantity and duration of services required. The total quantity of IaaS resources requested has no impact on the overall amount immediately. CSPs have the authority to increase or decrease current virtual machine rates, but they lack the authority to ask consumers how much they should pay or if they should spend more than the majority of customers. Maximize revenue for CSPs by selecting the best offer using a try-to-sell mechanism.

Model of auction pricing:

The decentralization idea in this segment enables Cluster-Coordinator (CCs) CSP organisations to gain complete control over their services in terms of success and assessment by the Main CSP. Cloud-based free enterprise leads to the emergence of future conflicts between IaaS customers and the CSPs specified by their CCs. This upcoming conflict (on both sides) must be resolved. We used auction methods and relied on the inherent features of distributed systems to develop our approaches. The auction technique guarantees that CSPs achieve the highest possible throughput of CCs within the methodological framework, resulting in financial benefits for all stakeholders. The auction approach increases the acceptance ratio, shortens the convergence time, eliminates repetition, and ensures the correctness of the resource allocation phase in the distributed method.

5.5 Summary

TABLE 5.1: COMPARISON OF MODELS

Criteria's	Model	
	RCG-IaaS	***HCIA***
Fifty-IaaS of Intra Bandwidth (Intra-Data Center Bandwidth (Mbps))	230	240
Hundred-IaaS of Intra Bandwidth (Gbps)	5.8	6
Hu Hundred-IaaS of Inter bandwidth (Mbps)	240	250
Ranges of profit depth-intervals from (α-ratio)	36.5 to 40	38 to 42
Variations impact of Intra/Inter-Data-Center Bandwidth (β-ratio)	0.036 to 0.070	0.038 to 0.076

As per the previous model i.e., RCG-IaaS (Regional-Column Generation IaaS provisioning) and the current model i.e., HCIA (Hierarchical-Cluster IaaS provisioning Architecture) the comparison of different parameters describes brief information related to model accuracy and best performance among two. In this the profit and blocking ratio intersects each other with optimum value of the bandwidth i.e., 240 here in Intra BW with 50 IaaS for HCIA, which is best for the model. After contrasting the α part in Fig.'s 5.2(a) & 5.2(b), we discovered that even the intersect points in the graph specifying the benefit breakpoint were between $\alpha = 42$ and $\alpha = 38$. The alpha indicates that the Intra-Data Center bandwidth was between two hundred and two hundred seventy-three megabits per second, corroborated by previous research. The profit cutoff for Inter-Data Center BW ranges between β=0.038 and 0.076, leading to Inter-Data Center amounts of between 5.75 and 6.95 Gbps. This defined the validity of our previous architecture (greater than 5 Gbps). 5.1 (c). To research the potential granularity of the cluster, Fig. 5.4 illustrates the exchange among net benefit (Eq. (one)) of the CSPs and distribution expense (Eq. (two)) of the amount of data centers in one cluster. Shown that, further than a cluster size of five-Data Centers, planned system increased income & lowered expense under high intensities. Even so, the pattern is flipped below a certain size.

Chapter6: 6.1 Implementation of Cluster-Based Framework

Demonstrating the test configuration with different settings, as previously shown. To evaluate the proposed clustered system against consolidated metrics, we selected an adequate network of 16 Data Centers distributed throughout India in four different clusters: East, West, and two clusters in the Middle, as shown in Figure 3.1. Each bunch is comprised of four Data Centers, each of which includes an indefinite number of VMs with different degrees of granularity according to Google Quality of Service groups (J. W. Charles Reiss, 2011). Additionally, each data centre makes use of a well-known device architecture (for example, FatTree) and an aggregated estimate of intra-Data Center system transfer speed based on different oversubscription esteems, as stated in (M. Al-Fares, 2008). The dispersed data centres are linked through the NSFNet topology, which acts as a backbone organisation segmented into the required, bunches (National Science Foundation Network, 2015). Each data centre is connected to the NSFNet through the hub located closest to its location. We concur that all NSFNet connections have a comparable bandwidth limit of 10Gbps. IaaS needs are generated using a C++ traffic generator module inspired by GT-ITM (K. C. E. Zegura & B. Bhattacharjee, 1996). The number of VMs allocated per demand is constantly between three and fifteen. Additionally, the required assets in each VM and the associated data transfer capacity requirement across VMs are evenly distributed between 300Mbps and 1Gbps.

The outstanding obligations are consistently generated between 50 and 100 solicitations for small measured IaaS remaining burdens with standard 300 VM and 500 association and between 120 and 200 solicitations for large measured IaaS residual loads with a usual relationship of 300 VM and 500. With typical seventeen hundred VM and twelve hundred association, the projected remaining loads are significant.

We used a cyclical strategy (A. Jarray& A. Karmouch, 2012). The preparatory period for re-enactment is divided into many stages p P. The cycle is adaptable in order to minimise the distortions inherent in sales and is characterised by an unusual number of solicitations gathered in small groups. The following illustrates this periodic procedure of distributing tiny clusters: Allow P to represent the configuration of configuration spans and R (0) to reflect the underlying configuration of IaaS needs. The following diagram depicts the organisation of IaaS requirements R(p) as defined by p1:

"R(p) = R (p − 1) + Rnew(p) − Rdrop(p)"

where R (p-1) represents the configuration of recognised IaaS needs at the conclusion of cycle p-1. Rnew(p) denotes the configuration of innovative methods, while Rdrop(p) is the configuration of consummation IaaS needs at the start of cycle p. The method simulates a real-world cloud environment and allows the model's productivity to be evaluated in the face of an increase in IaaS demand.

It is beneficial to conduct testing in immersed working circumstances to more easily evaluate the exhibition of IaaS provisioning methods. During routine system operation, joins are often provisioned to 30% to 50% of their capabilities (t. S. Jain, 2013). As a result, the solicitation generator is triggered, flooding the system with solicitations. We next conduct testing for 10 consecutive periods and record all installation results. This procedure is repeated many times and normal qualities are used in research. To demonstrate the methodology's flexibility, we increase the number of IaaS requests from one to one hundred. We repeat this method many times and use the expected results.

The matches are conducted using our C++-based discrete event test framework. We do extensive simulations using a variety of factors, including the number of IaaS requests, the number of clusters, the number of Data Centers in each group, and various oversubscription esteems. The queries were performed on an HP machine equipped with a 2.3 GHz Intel Core 5 CPU and 8 GB of RAM that was configured to run Windows 10 home single language and the IBM CPLEX solver (IBM LOG CPLEX Optimizer, 2015).

Performance Evaluation Metrics

We utilized the following exhibition measures to compare the presentation of Hierarchical-Cluster IaaS Architecture (HCIA) and Two-stage IaaS heuristic provisioning methods:

- Approval ratio: the percentage of recognised IaaS solicitations to all applications filed during a cycle.
- Data Center asset utilization: the proportion of resources (CPU, memory, storage, and transfer speed) that are fully used in the Data Center.
- Net benefit gained by the CSP: the total of the benefits earned by each CC in each party. Benefits are calculated based on the number of agreements obtained via successful solicitation, minus the cost of device characteristics and model-determined virtual machines.

Performance measure that is critical:

- Acceleration (Su): Acceleration gained by using several preparation hubs rather than a single hub.
- Efficiency (E): Percentage of the most intensive execution possible (in terms of speed or resource consumption) (percent)
- Elasticity (El): Dynamic interim management of auto-scaling assets with retaining load diversity

Productivity in the Cloud:

- Cloud QoS (Quality of Service): The rate at which a cloud management or benchmarking project is finished (percent)

- Service (Cost): The cost of cloud management was specified in terms of dollars per hour (Computing, Storage, and so on).
- Availability (A): The percentage of time during which the framework is available to do productive work.

6.2 Implementation of Cluster-Distributed Resource-Allocation Approach Through Geo-Distributed Data Center

We are presently inferring cooperation from our research into shill offering. The consequence of this area is that there is often an incentive for a prospective bidder to employ shills or an incentive for a prospective bidder partnership to consolidate.

To hone the investigation, it is valuable to kill the Competition Effect–which is even in a closeout for a single item. The link between the urge to split into distinct characters and the incentive for multiple personalities to combine has been studied in a variety of contexts, for example, split- and consolidate-proofness in planning issues. (Moulin, 2008)

A motivation for forming an alliance, and the urge to push transforms into a deterrent for forming an alliance. Both of these driving factors disappear simultaneously when additional material values are considered. One should bear in mind that there is some imbalance between peddler offering and combining in that, unlike peddler offering, combining does not result in unnecessary classifications among bidders; nevertheless, blending reduces the vender's income. We conclude the segment by noting that the problem of perfect conspiracy has much the same structure as the issue of optimal peddler providing at the moment (expecting the alliance can reallocate the merchandise after the closeout). If there are the same number of alliance members as goods for sale, this additional criterion cannot be met, and optimal plot degrades to ideal peddler offering.

As we have chosen the problem statement of addressing collusion in a cluster-distributed resource-allocation method as our starting point (Khaled Metwally, 2018). We used the IBM CPLEX LOG simulation (IBM ILOG CPLEX Optimizer, 2015) to demonstrate that whenever bidding occurs, the objective is to determine the most economical method of allocating assignments to bidders without collusion. The studies were carried out on a Hewlett-Packard computer equipped with a 2.3 GHz Intel-Core -5 processor and 8 GB of random-access memory running Windows 10 home single language and using the IBM CPLEX solver with C++ programming.

A few bidders are attempting to get a massive deal. The agreement is distinct. Into many responsibilities. Certain jobs are critical and must be awarded to the highest bidder. Others are not critical, and if they remain unassigned, a liability is imposed. Each bidder may make an offer for a subset of the undertakings, and each assignment may be optional or mandatory in the bid. While a discretionary assignment offer may be accepted separately, mandatory assignment offers are win or lose: mandatory assignments must be accepted in their whole or all will be rejected for each offer. The aim is to award the lowest-priced job to bidders.

6.3 Implementation of IaaS provisioning mathematical model: The Pricing Problems and its Optimal Solution

We are now debating ways to circumvent the HCIA model. To begin, the RPI must be setup with a collection of fake columns with zero income. For IAP questions, the top bounds are determined using a simple relaxation. The relaxation of the principal-IAP is accomplished by relaxing the constraint in Eq. (Nine) to c 2 [0;1]; c C. The measures to solution method are given by a dual nested loop procedure.

I) Configure RPI with zero-income dummy tables.

II) Solve Principal-LPR with CPLEX solver.

III) Solve the price dilemma using ideal dual variables.

IV) Fine-tune the price problem in order to identify a new column.

A) Whenever a positive cost-reduced column has been observed, link and re-optimize this segment with the principal-LPR. Otherwise, it is optimally solved by Principal-LPR.

B) We re-establish credibility constraints on λ to evaluate the principal-IAP integer solution and begin with CPLEX solver branch-and-bound. Notably, the conclusion of the principal-LPR solution means that the optimum upper limit for the principal-IAP solution has been reached. We must then have an integer solution to the IaaS provisioning issue in order to obtain an integer solution to Principal-IAP, reinstate the integrity limit, and address the principal-problem using a branch-and-bound method.

Chapter7: 7.1 Performance Measures: IaaS request Acceptance and Execution time

According to Table 7.1, the horizontal distribution represents the number of IaaS requests, while the vertical distribution represents IaaS provisioning approaches such as the proposed Hierarchical-Cluster IaaS provisioning Architecture (HCIA), as well as two additional approaches such as Regional Column Generation IaaS provisioning of Geographically dispersed clouds (RCG-IaaS) and Network-Aware Architecture as a service provisioning (NA-RA), The number of IaaS requests taken is typically 500, 600, 700, and 800, respectively, whereas the proposed HCIA approach accepted 440, 510, 623, and 720, which is significantly more than other approaches and also has a significantly higher acceptance ratio of 88 percent, 85 percent, 89 percent, and 90 percent, respectively, which is the highest acceptance ratio among other approaches.

If we consider alternative approaches, the accepted IaaS requests for the NA-RA approach are 405, 474, 560, and 640, respectively, with acceptance ratios of 81 percent, 79 percent, 80 percent, and 80 percent, which is less than the proposed HCIA approach, and the accepted IaaS requests for the RCG-IaaS approach are 360, 468, 553, and 632, respectively, with acceptance ratios of 72 percent, 78 percent, and 80 percent, respectively Thus, in terms of accepted IaaS requests and acceptance ratio, the Hierarchical-Cluster IaaS provisioning Architecture (HCIA) outperforms than other methods such as RCG-IaaS and NA-RA.

Table 7.1: HCIA: IaaS Request Acceptance

		Number of IaaS Requests			
IaaS Serving Approach		**500**	**600**	**700**	**800**
HCIA	# Accepted IaaS	440	510	623	720
	Acceptance Ratio	88%	85%	89%	90%
NA-RA	# Accepted IaaS	405	474	560	640
	Acceptance Ratio	81%	79%	80%	80%
RCG-IaaS	# Accepted IaaS	360	468	553	632
	Acceptance Ratio	72%	78%	79%	79%

Table 7.2: HCIA: Execution Time Analysis

	Measured Time (sec)			
# IaaS Requests	Load Time	Discovery Time	Composition Time	**Total Sim.**
500 IaaS	2.135	97.190	0.712	**17545.2**
600 IaaS	2.153	119.890	0.915	**21410.8**
700 IaaS	2.345	191.650	1.153	**26242.9**
800 IaaS	2.119	335.878	1.264	**31128.5**

According to Table 7.2, Hierarchical-Cluster IaaS provisioning Architecture (HCIA) requires less time, resulting in a more efficient ontology framework that considers expressivity. The performance of the suggested HCIA method is ensured by the short average discovery and composition times. On the other hand, the overall simulation duration represents the number of iterations achieved and the backtracking required by the algorithms relaxation conditions. Additionally, the expanding search area and the increasing number of IaaS requests significantly increase the average simulation duration. This finding broadens the solution's applicability to large datacenters and high-volume requirements. Additionally, the findings in Table 7.1 support this discovery, demonstrating that the acceptance ratio of the suggested method falls significantly as the number of IaaS requests increases, despite the fact that HCIA achieved a high acceptance ratio. High acceptance ratio and accepted IaaS requests among the benchmarks.

7.2 Cheapest Assignment of Resources Through Bidders

The thesis demonstrates the cheapest allocation of resources through bidders by simulating combinatorial sell-offs using the shill offering concept in the V.C.G. scheme. Shill offering is a technique in which a single leader participates in bartering under a variety of guises. Using this approach, we've used Task Set, Tasks, and Task Penalty (if the cost is -1, the task must be allocated) as inputs to the system and determined the most cost-effective way of allocating assignments to bidders, as shown in Figure 4.4. (g).

The Figures 4.4 (a) and (b) show Peak Time of cheapest assignment and award & avoid data in the form of scripting log. Figure 4.4 (c) shows the bidding solution with result data and Figure 4.4 (d) shows the avoid solution on DOcplexcloud. Figure 4.4 (e) and (f) shows the award solution, avoided bid on DOcplexcloud. The DOcplexcloud is a decision optimization on cloud that solve optimization problems on the cloud. This shows that after applying assignment constraint, each task must be assigned to a bid then after it gives optimal solution as a cheapest assignment to the tasks to the bidders without any collusion.

7.3 Optimal Solution of IaaS Provisioning Through Intra and Inter Bandwidth of Data centers

As with the previous model, RCG-IaaS (Regional-Column Generation IaaS provisioning), and the current model, HCIA (Hierarchical-Cluster IaaS provisioning Architecture), the comparison of various parameters provides concise information about the model's accuracy and best performance when compared to the previous model.

Profit and blocking ratios meet at the optimal bandwidth value, which in this case is 240 in Intra BW with 50 IaaS for HCIA, which is optimal for the model. After comparing the sections in Figures 5.2(a) and 5.2(b), we found that even the intersect points in the graph defining the benefit breakpoint were between = 42 and = 38. The alpha suggests that the Intra-DC BW was between 230 and 273 megabits per second, which is consistent with prior studies. Profitability thresholds for Inter-Data Center BW vary between 0.038 and 0.076, resulting in Inter-Data Center bandwidths of between 5.75 and 6.95 Gbps. This established the correctness of our prior design (greater than 5 Gbps). 5.1.1 (c). To investigate the cluster's possible granularity, Fig. 5.3 depicts the exchange between the net benefit (Eq. 1) of the CSPs and the distribution cost (Eq. 2) of the number of data centers in a cluster. It was shown that, beyond a cluster size of five data centers, a designed system boosted revenue and decreased cost at high number of IaaS requests.

Chapter 8: 8.1 Introduction

This research offers a cluster-based architecture for IaaS that allows consumers to access professionally hosted high-performance computing applications while also allowing CSPs to optimize their resource utilization. The goal is to impose necessary performance criteria such as speed, efficiency, flexibility, and cloud productivity, as well as cloud quality of service, service cost, and availability. Additionally, we would enhance geodata centers capacity to provide products to customers more quickly and efficiently than was previously possible using traditional methods. Nonetheless, huge data centres become economically unproductive when their expenses increase in lockstep with the expansion of current large-scale application needs. Currently, we have a defined framework for Infrastructure-as-a-Service agreements that provides a cost-effective, flexible, and service-quality-assured method for encouraging massive expansion solicitations across geographically dispersed server farms. The structure joins two distributed approach divisions that are comparable, distinct radical, and stated, and that make effective use of monetary representations. There are many methods, each with a very advantageous response to the adaptability and recognition of the complex nature of contemporary processes. Finally, cost effectiveness has been ascribed to a well-distributed architecture in light of new compensation requirements for Cloud Service Providers. Preoccupation yields demonstrate the bid job's productivity by matching the future profits of proposed courses of action to the client's requirements, all while producing unequalled resource utilisation and Cloud Service Provider (CSP) payoffs. Additionally, we proposed a method for cluster-distributed resource sharing. We are using the Vickrey-Clarke-Groves (VCG) framework to get a deeper understanding of inquisitiveness and misrepresentation in a cluster-distributed resource allocation method through geo-distributed data centres. Additionally, we can demonstrate this via simulation, in which a large number of bidders negotiate a large transaction. The transaction is divided into multiple assignments. Certain tasks are critical and must be delegated. Others are not essential and, if left unassigned, incur a penalty. The objective is to determine the most cost-effective method of allocating assignments to bidders. Thus, no collusion between such bidders during the bidding process is permitted.

Deployment of IaaS applications is one of the most interesting features of cloud infrastructure services, since it allows the provisioning of sophisticated applications. IaaS, or Infrastructure as a Service, is the supply of essential computer infrastructure for the Internet-based deployment of commercial applications. This includes components such as storage, hardware, servers, and networking. IaaS often relocates the physical architecture of IT applications offshore and a service provider gives customers access to a virtualized environment with processing services. We have concentrated on price issues and the optimum approach that would provide the greatest returns.

8.2 Conclusion

The method to IaaS provisioning HCIA stated that the entire IaaS provisioning is dynamic and places a greater focus on other performance criteria such as elasticity, quality of service, service cost, and availability, achieving a higher level than the previous two methods (RCG-IaaS, & NA-RA). As a result, the HCIA technique outperforms all other described approaches.

The cluster-distributed method to resource allocation lowers the complexity of resource allocation and simplifies the distribution of jobs to bidders as cheaply as feasible without introducing collusion into the system. Collaborative bidding between several bidders for a single offer has been eliminated in this method by implementing the notion of shill bidding in a double-sided vendue (auction) using the VCG mechanism. Additionally, this method optimizes resource allocation via many bidders for a single offer.

The IaaS provisioning method outlined by HCIA is dynamic and places a greater focus on performance metrics such as blocking ratio, profit, and intra/inter bandwidths, demonstrating the greatest degree of performance compared to the other approaches discussed before (RCG-IaaS). As a result, the HCIA technique is superior than other specified methods in terms of performance.

8.3 Future Scope

The system developed would be extended to host cloud-based smartphone applications, and its effectiveness in a changing environment can be determined. The work would be expanded in the mobile cloud applications with the purpose of enhancing the cloud environment's ability to deal with new trends in resource allocation and provisioning from many clusters. In the future, mobile cloud applications will use resource assignment with 100% efficiency and precision. As a result, the whole study would be moved to the mobile cloud environment in the future to further improve performance.

BIBLIOGRAPHY

A. Ahmed, Z. M. Faten, L. Rami, B. Raouf, and P. Guy, "Greenhead: Virtual data center embedding across distributed infrastructures," IEEE Transactions on Cloud Computing, vol. 1, no. 1, January-June 2013.

A. Archer, J. Feigenbaum, A. Krishnamurthy, R. Sami, and S. Shenker. Ap- proximation and collusion in multicast cost sharing. Games and Economic Behavior, 47(1):pages 36-71, April 2004.

A. Archer, J. Feigenbaum, A. Krishnamurthy, R. Sami, and S. Shenker, 2003. Approximation and collusion in multicast cost sharing. Games and Economic Behavior. To appear.

A. Belbekkouche, M. M. Hasan, and A. Karmouch, "Resource Discovery and Alloca- tion in Network Virtualization," Communications Surveys Tutorials, IEEE, vol. 14, no. 4, pp. 1114–1128, Fourth 2012.

A. Beloglazov, J. Abawajy, and R. Buyya, "Energy-aware Resource Allocation Heuristics for Efficient Management of Data Centers for Cloud Computing," Future Gener. Comput. Syst., vol. 28, no. 5, pp. 755–768, May 2012.

A. Darabseh, M. Al-Ayyoub, Y. Jararweh, E. Benkhelifa, M. Vouk, and A. Rindos, "Sddc: A software defined datacenter experimental framework," in Future Internet of Things and Cloud (FiCloud), 2015 3rd International Conference on, Aug 2015, pp. 189–194.

A. Greenberg, J. R. Hamilton, N. Jain, S. Kandula, C. Kim, P. Lahiri, D. A. Maltz, P. Patel, and S. Sengupta, "VL2: A Scalable and Flexible Data Center Network," in Proceedings of the ACM SIGCOMM 2009 Conference on Data Communication, ser. SIGCOMM '09. New York, NY, USA: ACM, 2009, pp. 51–62.

A. Greenberg, J. R. Hamilton, N. Jain, S. Kandula, C. Kim, P. Lahiri, D. A. Maltz, P. Patel, and S. Sengupta, "VL2: A Scalable and Flexible Data Center Network," in Proceedings of the ACM SIGCOMM 2009 Conference on Data Communication, ser. SIGCOMM '09. New York, NY, USA: ACM, 2009, pp. 51–62.

A. Jarray and A. Karmouch, "Periodical auctioning for QoS aware virtual network embedding," in 2012 IEEE 20th International Workshop on Quality of Service (IWQoS), June 2012, pp. 1–4.

A. Rai, R. Bhagwan, and S. Guha, "Generalized Resource Allocation for the Cloud," in Proceedings of the Third ACM Symposium on Cloud Computing, ser. SoCC '12. New York, NY, USA: ACM, 2012, pp. 15:1–15:12.

Apache CloudStack, https://cloudstack.apache.org/, Last visited: July 2015.

Ausubel and Milgrom: "The Lovely but Lonely Vickrey Auction," in Combinatorial Auctions, ed. by P. Crampton, Y. Shoham, and R. Steinberg, pp. 17–40. MIT Press, 2006.

B. Jennings and R. Stadler, "Resource Management in Clouds: Survey and Research Challenges," Journal of Network and Systems Management, pp. 1–53, 2014.

B. Kantarci and H. Mouftah, "Inter-data center network dimen- sioning under time-of-use pricing," IEEE Transactions on Cloud Computing, vol. 4, pp. 402–414, 2017.

B. Li, J. Li, J. Huai, T. Wo, Q. Li, and L. Zhong, "EnaCloud: An Energy-Saving Application Live Placement Approach for Cloud Computing Environments," in Cloud Computing, 2009. CLOUD '09. IEEE International Conference on, Sept 2009, pp. 17–24.

C. Lee, P. Wang, and D. Niyato, "A real-time group auction system for efficient allocation of cloud internet applications," IEEE Transactions on Services Computing, vol. 8, no. 2, pp. 251–268, March 2015.

C. Clark, K. Fraser, S. Hand, J. G. Hansen, E. Jul, C. Limpach, I. Pratt, and A. Warfield, "Live Migration of Virtual Machines," in Proceedings of the 2Nd Con- ference on Symposium on Networked Systems Design & Implementation - Volume 2, ser. NSDI'05. Berkeley, CA, USA: USENIX Association, 2005, pp. 273–286.

C. Guo, G. Lu, D. Li, H. Wu, X. Zhang, Y. Shi, C. Tian, Y. Zhang, and S. Lu, "BCube: A High Performance, Server-centric Network Architecture for Modular Data Centers," in Proceedings of the ACM SIGCOMM 2009 Conference on Data Communication, ser. SIGCOMM '09. New York, NY, USA: ACM, 2009, pp. 63–74.

C. Guo, G. Lu, H. J. Wang, S. Yang, C. Kong, P. Sun, W. Wu, and Y. Zhang, "SecondNet: a data center network virtualization architecture with bandwidth guar- antees." in CoNEXT, J. C. de Oliveira, M. Ott, T. G. Griffin, and M. M′edard, Eds. ACM, 2010, p. 15.

C. Lee, P. Wang, and D. Niyato, "A Real-Time Group Auction System for Efficient Allocation of Cloud Internet Applications," Services Computing, IEEE Transactions on, vol. 8, no. 2, pp. 251–268, March 2015.

C. Leiserson, "Fat-trees: Universal networks for hardware-efficient supercomputing," Computers, IEEE Transactions on, vol. C-34, no. 10, pp. 892–901, Oct 1985.

C. Papagianni, A. Leivadeas, S. Papavassiliou, V. Maglaris, C. Cervello-Pastor, and A. Monje, "On the optimal allocation of virtual resources in cloud computing networks," IEEE Transactions on Computers, vol. 62, no. 6, pp. 1060–1071, June 2013.

C. Vecchiola, S. Pandey, and R. Buyya, "High-performance cloud computing: A view of scientific applications," in 2009 10th International Symposium on Pervasive Systems, Algorithms, and Networks (ISPAN), Dec 2009, pp. 4–16.

Cramton, P. Spectrum Auction Design. Rev Ind Organ 42, 161–190 (2013). https://doi.org/10.1007/s11151-013-9376-x.

D. Abts and B. Felderman, “A Guided Tour of Data-center Networking,” Commun. ACM, vol. 55, no. 6, pp. 44–51, Jun. 2012.

D. Ardagna, S. Casolari, and B. Panicucci, “Flexible distributed capacity allocation and load redirect algorithms for cloud systems,” in Cloud Computing (CLOUD), 2011 IEEE International Conference on, July 2011, pp. 163–170.

D. Breitgand and A. Glikson, “Global enterprise cloud transfor- mation: Centralize, distribute or federate?” in 2013 IFIP/IEEE In- ternational Symposium on Integrated Network Management (IM 2013), May 2013, pp. 892–895.

D. Chisnall, The Definitive Guide to the Xen Hypervisor, 1st ed. Upper Saddle River, NJ, USA: Prentice Hall Press, 2007.

D. Gale and L. S. Shapley, “College Admissions and the Stability of Marriage,” The American Mathematical Monthly, vol. 69, no. 1, pp. pp. 9–15, 1962.

D. Irwin, P. Shenoy, E. Cecchet, and M. Zink, “Resource management in data- intensive clouds: Opportunities and challenges,” in Local and Metropolitan Area Networks (LANMAN), 2010 17th IEEE Workshop on, May 2010, pp. 1–6.

D. Jayasinghe, C. Pu, T. Eilam, M. Steinder, I. Whally, and E. Snible, “Improving Performance and Availability of Services Hosted on IaaS Clouds with Structural Constraint-Aware Virtual Machine Placement,” in Services Computing (SCC), 2011 IEEE International Conference on, July 2011, pp. 72–79.

D. Nurmi, R. Wolski, C. Grzegorczyk, G. Obertelli, S. Soman, L. Youseff, and D. Zagorodnov, “The Eucalyptus Open-Source Cloud-Computing System,” in Pro- ceedings of the 2009 9th IEEE/ACM International Symposium on Cluster Computing and the Grid, ser. CCGRID '09. Washington, DC, USA: IEEE Computer Society, 2009, pp. 124–131.

D. S. Marcon, R. R. Oliveira, L. P. Gaspary, and M. P. Barcellos, "Datacenter networks and relevant standards," in Cloud Services, Networking, and Management. John Wiley & Sons, Inc, 2015, pp. 73–104.

D. Talia, "Clouds for Scalable Big Data Analytics," Computer, vol. 46, no. 5, pp. 98–101, May 2013.

E. G. Coffman, Jr., M. R. Garey, and D. S. Johnson, "Approximation Algorithms for NP-hard Problems," D. S. Hochbaum, Ed. Boston, MA, USA: PWS Publishing Co., 1997, ch. Approximation Algorithms for Bin Packing: A Survey, pp. 46–93.

F. Abbaspourtorbati and M. Zima, "The Swiss Reserve Market: Stochastic Programming in Practice," in IEEE Transactions on Power Systems, vol. 31, no. 2, pp. 1188-1194, March 2016, doi: 10.1109/TPWRS.2015.2415467.

F. Gomez-Folgar, A. Garcia-Loureiro, T. F. Pena, and R. Valin, "Performance of the CloudStack KVM Pod Primary Storage Under NFS Version 3," in Proceedings of the 2012 IEEE 10th International Symposium on Parallel and Distributed Processing with Applications, ser. ISPA '12. Washington, DC, USA: IEEE Computer Society, 2012, pp. 845–846.

F. Hao, T. V. Lakshman, S. Mukherjee, and H. Song, "Enhancing dynamic cloud- based services using network virtualization," SIGCOMM Comput. Commun. Rev., vol. 40, no. 1, pp. 67–74, Jan. 2010.

F. Liu, J. Tong, J. Mao, R. Bohn, J. Messina, L. Badger, and D. Leaf, NIST Cloud Computing Reference Architecture: Recommendations of the National Institute of

Standards and Technology (Special Publication 500-292). USA: CreateSpace Independent Publishing Platform, 2012.

F. Samuel, M. Chowdhury, and R. Boutaba, "Polyvine: policy- based virtual network embedding across multiple domains," Jour- nal of Internet Services and Applications, vol. 4, no. 1, 2013.

F. Wuhib, R. Stadler, and H. Lindgren, "Dynamic resource allocation with management objectives: Implementation for an openstack cloud," in Proceedings of the 8th International Conference on Network and Service Management, ser. CNSM '12. Laxenburg, Austria, Austria: International Federation for Information Processing, 2013, pp. 309–315.

G. Feng, S. Garg, R. Buyya, and W. Li, "Revenue Maximization Using Adaptive Resource Provisioning in Cloud Computing Environments," in Proceedings of the 2012 ACM/IEEE 13th International Conference on Grid Computing, ser. GRID '12. Washington, DC, USA: IEEE Computer Society, 2012, pp. 192–200.

G. Jung, K. Joshi, M. Hiltunen, R. Schlichting, and C. Pu, "Generating Adaptation Policies for Multi-tier Applications in Consolidated Server Environments," in Au- tonomic Computing, 2008. ICAC '08. International Conference on, June 2008, pp. 23–32.

GREEN, J., AND J.-J. LAFFONT: "Characterization of Satisfactory Mechanisms for the Revelation of Preferences for Public Goods," Econometrica, 45, 427–438, 1977.

Gupta. Shashi Kant, Khanum. Mohammadi Akheela, "Implementing a cluster-based approach for auto-scalable IaaS provisioning in Geo-distributed Data Centers," International Journal of Advanced Science and Technology, vol. 29, issue 3. April 2020, pp. 7205–7217.

Gupta. Shashi Kant, Khanum. Mohammadi Akheela, “A Review: Distributed Auction-Based Framework v/s Cluster-Based Framework for Auto Scalable IaaS Provisioning in Geo-Data Centers,” International Journal of Computer Sciences and Engineering, vol. 7, issue 2. Feb 2019, pp. 469–476.

H. Ballani, P. Costa, T. Karagiannis, and A. Rowstron, “Towards Predictable Dat- acenter Networks,” in Proceedings of the ACM SIGCOMM 2011 Conference, ser. SIGCOMM ’11. New York, NY, USA: ACM, 2011, pp. 242–253.

H. Kim and N. Feamster, “Improving network management with software defined networking,” Communications Magazine, IEEE, vol. 51, no. 2, pp. 114–119, February 2013.

H. Liu, H. Jin, X. Liao, L. Hu, and C. Yu, “Live Migration of Virtual Machine Based on Full System Trace and Replay,” in Proceedings of the 18th ACM International Symposium on High Performance Distributed Computing, ser. HPDC ’09. New York, NY, USA: ACM, 2009, pp. 101–110.

H. Rodrigues, J. R. Santos, Y. Turner, P. Soares, and D. Guedes, “Gatekeeper: Supporting Bandwidth Guarantees for Multi-tenant Datacenter Networks,” in Pro- ceedings of the 3rd Conference on I/O Virtualization, ser. WIOV’11. Berkeley, CA, USA: USENIX Association, 2011, pp. 6–6.

H. Xu and B. Li, “Dynamic Cloud Pricing for Revenue Maximization,” Cloud Com- puting, IEEE Transactions on, vol. 1, no. 2, pp. 158–171, July 2013.

H. Xu and B. Li, “Egalitarian stable matching for VM migration in cloud comput- ing,” in Computer Communications Workshops (INFOCOM WKSHPS), 2011 IEEE Conference on, April 2011, pp. 631–636.

HOLMSTRom, B.: "Groves Schemes on Restricted Domains," Econometrica, 55, 303–328, 1979.

IFAC-PapersOnLine, ISSN: 2405-8963, Vol: 50, Issue: 1, Page: 189-194, July 2017.

I. Fajjari, M. Ayari, and G. Pujolle, "VN-SLA: A Virtual Network Specification Schema for Virtual Network Provisioning," in Networks (ICN), 2010 Ninth Interna- tional Conference on, April 2010, pp. 337–342.

I. Fajjari, N. Aitsaadi, G. Pujolle, and H. Zimmermann, "VNR Algorithm: A Greedy Approach For Virtual Networks Reconfigurations," in VNR Algorithm : A Greedy Approach For Virtual Networks Reconfigurations. Houston, E´tats-Unis: IEEE, 2011, pp. 6–11.

I. Houidi, W. Louati, and D. Zeghlache, "A distributed virtual network mapping algorithm," in Communications, 2008. ICC '08. IEEE International Conference on, May 2008, pp. 5634–5640.

I. Houidi, W. Louati, D. Zeghlache, and S. Baucke, "Virtual Resource Description and Clustering for Virtual Network Discovery," in Communications Workshops, 2009. ICC Workshops 2009. IEEE International Conference on, June 2009, pp. 1–6..

I. Houidi, W. Louati, W. B. Ameur, and D. Zeghlache, "Virtual net- work provisioning across multiple substrate networks," Computer Networks, vol. 55, no. 4, pp. 1011 – 1023, 2011, special Issue on Architectures and Protocols for the Future Internet.

IBM LOG CPLEX Optimizer, http://www 01.ibm.com/software/integration/optimization/cplex-optimizer/, Last visited: July 2015.

IBM ILOG CPLEX Optimizer, http://www-01.ibm.com/software/integration/optimization/cplex-optimizer/, Last visited: July 2015.

Itai Sher, 2012. "Optimal shill bidding in the VCG mechanism," Economic Theory, Springer;Society for the Advancement of Economic Theory (SAET), vol. 50(2), pages 341-387, June.

J. Araujo Wickboldt, L. Zambenedetti Granville, F. Schneider, D. Dudkowski, and J. Carapinha and J. Jim´enez, "Network Virtualization: A View from the Bottom," in Proceedings of the 1st ACM Workshop on Virtualized Infrastructure Systems and Architectures, ser. VISA '09. New York, NY, USA: ACM, 2009, pp. 73–80.

J. Carapinha, P. Feil, P. Weissmann, S. E. Thorsteinsson, c. Etemo˘glu, O. Ingp´orsson, S. C¸ ift¸ci, and M. Melo, "Network Virtualization - Opportunities and Challenges for Operators," in Proceedings of the Third Future Internet Conference on Future Internet, ser. FIS'10. Berlin, Heidelberg: Springer-Verlag, 2010, pp. 138–147.

J. F. Joan A. Garc´ıa et al., "Logical Infrastructure Composition Layer, the GEY- SERS Holistic Approach for Infrastructure Virtualisation.", 2013.

J. He, R. Zhang-shen, Y. Li, C. yen Lee, J. Rexford, and M. Chiang, "DaVinci: Dynamically Adaptive Virtual Networks for a Customized Internet," in in Proc. CoNEXT, 2008.

J. Kang and K. Sim, "Cloudle: An Ontology-Enhanced Cloud Service Search En- gine," in Web Information Systems Engineering – WISE 2010 Workshops, ser. Lec- ture Notes in Computer Science, D. Chiu, L. Bellatreche, H. Sasaki, H.-f. Leung, S.-C. Cheung, H. Hu, and J. Shao, Eds. Springer Berlin Heidelberg, 2011, vol. 6724, pp. 416–427.

J. Shamsi, M. A. Khojaye, and M. A. Qasmi, "Data-intensive cloud computing: Requirements, expectations, challenges, and solutions," J. Grid Comput., vol. 11, no. 2, pp. 281–310, Jun. 2013.

J. Turner and D. Taylor, "Diversifying the Internet," in Global Telecommunications Conference, 2005. GLOBECOM '05. IEEE, vol. 2, Dec 2005, pp. 6 pp.–760.

J.W. Charles Reiss, "Google cluster-usage traces: format+schema,"Tech. Rep., 2011.

J.Y. Shin, B. Wong, and E. G. Sirer, "Small-world datacenters," in Proceedings of the 2Nd ACM Symposium on Cloud Computing, ser. SOCC '11. New York, NY, USA: ACM, 2011, pp. 2:1–2:13.

Jackson, M. O. (2000). Mechanism theory. In the Encyclopedia of Life Support Systems. EOLSS Publishers. Jackson, 2000

K. M. Metwally, A. Jarray, and A. Karmouch, "A Cost-Efficient QoS-Aware model for cloud IaaS resource allocation n large datacenters," in 4th IEEE international Conference on Cloud Networking, Niagara Falls, Canada, Oct. 2015.

K. A. Scarfone, M. P. Souppaya, and P. Hoffman, "SP 800-125. Guide to Security for Full Virtualization Technologies," Gaithersburg, MD, United States, Tech. Rep., 2011.

K. C. E. Zegura and B. Bhattacharjee, "How to model an nternet-work," n Proceedings of IEEE infocom, 1996, pp. 594–602.

K. Chard, K. Bubendorfer, and P. Komisarczuk, "High Occupancy Resource Allo- cation for Grid and Cloud Systems, a Study with DRIVE," in Proceedings of the 19th ACM International Symposium on High Performance Distributed Computing, ser. HPDC '10. New York, NY, USA: ACM, 2010, pp. 73–84.

K. M. Metwally, A. Jarray, and A. Karmouch, "A Cost-Efficient QoS-Aware model for cloud IaaS resource allocation in large dat- acenters," in 4th IEEE International Conference on Cloud Networking, Niagara Falls, Canada, Oct. 2015.

K. Sripanidkulchai, S. Sahu, Y. Ruan, A. Shaikh, and C. Dorai, "Are Clouds Ready for Large Distributed Applications?" SIGOPS Oper. Syst. Rev., vol. 44, no. 2, pp. 18–23, Apr. 2010.

K. yin Chen, Y. Xu, K. Xi, and H. Chao, "Intelligent virtual machine placement for cost efficiency in geo-distributed cloud systems," in Communications (ICC), 2013 IEEE International Conference on, June 2013, pp. 3498–3503.

Khaled Metwally, Abdallah Jarray, Ahmad Karmouch, "A distributed auction-based framework for scalable IaaS provisioning in geo-data centers," IEEE transactions on cloud computing, 2018.

Khaled Metwally, Abdallah Jarray, and Ahmed Karmouch, "A Distributed Auction-based Framework for Scalable IaaS Provisioning in Geo-Data Centers" IEEE transactions on cloud computing, Oct 2018, pp. 1-14

Krishna, V. (2002). Sealed-bid (Vickrey) auction, Auction Theory. Academic Press.

L. Hu, K. D. Ryu, M. Silva, and K. Schwan, "v-Bundle: Flexible Group Resource Offerings in Clouds," in Distributed Computing Systems (ICDCS), 2012 IEEE 32nd International Conference on, June 2012, pp. 406–415.

L. jie Zhang and Q. Zhou, "CCOA: Cloud Computing Open Architecture," in International Conference on Web Services, 2009, pp. 607–616.

L. Popa, S. Ratnasamy, G. Iannaccone, A. Krishnamurthy, and I. Stoica, "A Cost Comparison of Datacenter Network Architectures," in Proceedings of the 6th International COnference, ser. Co-NEXT '10. New York, NY, USA: ACM, 2010, pp. 16:1–16:12.

L. Shi, B. Butler, D. Botvich, and B. Jennings, "Provisioning of requests for virtual machine sets with placement constraints in IaaS clouds," in Integrated Network Man- agement (IM 2013), 2013 IFIP/IEEE International Symposium on, May 2013, pp. 499–505.

L. Wu, S. Garg, and R. Buyya, "SLA-Based Resource Allocation for Software as a Service Provider (SaaS) in Cloud Computing Environments," in Cluster, Cloud and Grid Computing (CCGrid), 2011 11th IEEE/ACM International Symposium on, May 2011, pp. 195–204.

M. E. Ubbecke and J. Desrosiers, "Selected topics in column generation," Operational Research, vol. 53, pp. 1007–1023, 2005.

M. Al-Fares, A. Loukissas, and A. Vahdat, "A scalable, commodity data center network architecture," in Proceedings of the ACM SIGCOMM 2008 Conference on Data Communication, ser. SIGCOMM '08. ACM, 2008, pp. 63–74.

M. Alicherry and T. Lakshman, "Network aware resource allocation in distributed clouds," in INFOCOM, 2012 Proceedings IEEE, March 2012, pp. 963–971.

M. Brunner, "Rethinking cloud platforms: Network-aware flexible resource allocation in IaaS clouds," in Integrated Network Management (IM 2013), 2013 IFIP/IEEE International Symposium on, May 2013, pp. 450–456.

M. Chowdhury, M. Rahman, and R. Boutaba, "ViNEYard: Virtual Network Em- bedding Algorithms With Coordinated Node and Link Mapping," Networking, IEEE/ACM Transactions on, vol. 20, no. 1, pp. 206 –219, feb. 2012.

M. E. Ubbecke and J. Desrosiers, "Selected topics in column generation," Operational Research, vol. 53, pp. 1007–1023, 2005.

M. F. Bari, R. Boutaba, P. R. R. Esteves, L. Granville, M. Podlesny, M. G. Rabbani, Q. Zhang, and M. Zhani, "Data Center Network Virtualization: A Survey." IEEE Communications Surveys and Tutorials, vol. 15, no. 2, pp. 909–928, 2013.

M. Ghijsen, J. Van der Ham, P. Grosso, and C. De Laat, "Towards an Infrastruc- ture Description Language for Modeling Computing Infrastructures," in Parallel and Distributed Processing with Applications (ISPA), 2012 IEEE 10th International Symposium on, July 2012, pp. 207–214.

M. Hadji and D. Zeghlache, "Minimum Cost Maximum Flow Algorithm for Dynamic Resource Allocation in Clouds," in Cloud Computing (CLOUD), 2012 IEEE 5th International Conference on, June 2012, pp. 876–882.

M. Nelson, B.-H. Lim, and G. Hutchins, "Fast Transparent Migration for Virtual Machines," in Proceedings of the Annual Conference on USENIX Annual Technical Conference, ser. ATEC '05. Berkeley, CA, USA: USENIX Association, 2005, pp. 25–25.

M. R. Hines and K. Gopalan, "Post-copy Based Live Virtual Machine Migration Us- ing Adaptive Pre-paging and Dynamic Self-ballooning," in Proceedings of the 2009 ACM SIGPLAN/SIGOPS International Conference on Virtual Execution Environ- ments, ser. VEE '09. New York, NY, USA: ACM, 2009, pp. 51–60.

Milgrom: Putting Auction Theory to Work. Cambridge University Press, 2004.

MOULIN, H.: "Proportional Scheduling, Split-Proofness, and Merge-Proofness,"Games and Economic Behavior, 63, 567–587, 2008.

N. Bobroff, A. Kochut, and K. Beaty, "Dynamic Placement of Virtual Machines for Managing SLA Violations," in Integrated Network Management, 2007. IM '07. 10th IFIP/IEEE International Symposium on, May 2007, pp. 119–128.

N. Chowdhury and R. Boutaba, "Network virtualization: state of the art and research challenges," Communications Magazine, IEEE, vol. 47, no. 7, pp. 20–26, July 2009.

N. M. K. Chowdhury and R. Boutaba, "A survey of network virtualization," Comput. Netw., vol. 54, no. 5, pp. 862–876, Apr. 2010.

National Science Foundation Network, http://www.nsf.gov/, Last visited: July 2015.

O. Biran, A. Corradi, M. Fanelli, L. Foschini, A. Nus, D. Raz, and E. Silvera, "A Stable Network-Aware VM Placement for Cloud Systems," in Cluster, Cloud and Grid Computing (CCGrid), 2012 12th IEEE/ACM International Symposium on, May 2012, pp. 498–506.

OpenNebula Home Page, http://www.opennebula.org/, Last visited: July 2015.

Optimal shill bidding in the VCG mechanism, Itai Sher University of Minnesota, September 3, 2010.

P. Bod´ık, I. Menache, M. Chowdhury, P. Mani, D. A. Maltz, and I. Stoica, "Surviving Failures in Bandwidth-constrained Datacenters," in Proceedings of the ACM SIGCOMM 2012 Conference on Applications, Technologies, Architectures, and Protocols for Computer Communication, ser. SIGCOMM '12. New York, NY, USA: ACM, 2012, pp. 431–442.

P. R. Lewis, F. Faniyi, R. Bahsoon, and X. Yao, "Markets and Clouds: Adaptive and Resilient Computational Resource Allocation inspired by Economics," in Adaptive, Dynamic, and Resilient Systems, N. Suri and G. Cabri, Eds. Boca Raton, FL, USA: CRC Press, 2014.

Q. Duan, Y. Yan, and A. Vasilakos, "A Survey on Service-Oriented Network Virtualization Toward Convergence of Networking and Cloud Computing," Network and Service Management, IEEE Transactions on, vol. 9, no. 4, pp. 373–392, December 2012.

Q. Li, Q. Hao, L. Xiao, and Z. Li, "Adaptive Management of Virtualized Resources in Cloud Computing Using Feedback Control," in Information Science and Engineering (ICISE), 2009 1st International Conference on, Dec 2009, pp. 99–102.

Q. Zhang, and M. Zhani, "Data Center Network Virtualization: A Survey." IEEE Communications Surveys and Tutorials, vol. 15, no. 2, pp. 909–928, 2013.

Q. Zhang, L. Cheng, and R. Boutaba, "Cloud computing: state-of-the-art and re- search challenges," Journal of Internet Services and Applications, vol. 1, no. 1, pp. 7–18, 2010.

Q. Zhang, Q. Zhu, M. Zhani, and R. Boutaba, "Dynamic service placement in geographically distributed clouds," in 2012 IEEE 32nd International Conference on Distributed Computing Systems

Q. Zhang, Q. Zhu, M. Zhani, and R. Boutaba, "Dynamic Service Placement in Geographically Distributed Clouds," in Distributed Computing Systems (ICDCS), 2012 IEEE 32nd International Conference on, June 2012, pp. 526–535.

R. Bless and C. Werle, "Control Plane Issues in the 4WARD Network Virtualization Architecture," Electronic Communications of the EASST, vol. 17, 2009.

R. Gupta, S. Bose, S. Sundarrajan, M. Chebiyam, and A. Chakrabarti, "A Two Stage Heuristic Algorithm for Solving the Server Consolidation Problem with Item-Item and Bin-Item Incompatibility Constraints," in Services Computing, 2008. SCC '08. IEEE International Conference on, vol. 2, July 2008, pp. 39–46.

R. Mian and P. Martin, “Executing Data-Intensive Workloads in a Cloud,” in Proceedings of the 2012 12th IEEE/ACM International Symposium on Cluster, Cloud and Grid Computing (Ccgrid 2012), ser. CCGRID ’12. Washington, DC, USA: IEEE Computer Society, 2012, pp. 758–763.

R. Moreno-Vozmediano, R. Montero, and I. Llorente, “Key Challenges in Cloud Computing: Enabling the Future Internet of Services,” Internet Computing, IEEE, vol. 17, no. 4, pp. 18–25, July 2013.

R. Tudoran, A. Costan, R. Wang, L. Bouge, and G. Antoniu, “Bridging data in the clouds: An environment-aware system for geographically distributed data transfers,” in 2014 14th IEEE/ACM International Symposium on Cluster, Cloud and Grid Computing (CCGrid), May 2014, pp. 92–101.

Robert W. Day, Peter Cramton, (2012). “Quadratic Core-Selecting Payment Rules for Combinatorial Auctions”, Vol.:60, No.:3, pp. iii-738, https://doi.org/10.1287/opre.1110.1024

ROTHKoPF, M.: “Thirteen Reasons why the Vickrey-Clarke-Groves Process is Not Practical,” Operations Research, 55, 191–197, 2007.

S. Akoush, R. Sohan, A. Rice, A. Moore, and A. Hopper, “Predicting the Performance of Virtual Machine Migration,” in Modeling, Analysis Simulation of Computer and Telecommunication Systems (MASCOTS), 2010 IEEE International Symposium on, Aug 2010, pp. 37–46.

S. Bazarbayev, M. Hiltunen, K. Joshi, W. Sanders, and R. Schlichting, “Content- Based Scheduling of Virtual Machines (VMs) in the Cloud,” in Distributed Computing Systems (ICDCS), 2013 IEEE 33rd International Conference on, July 2013, pp. 93– 101.

S. Ghasemi-Falavarjani, M. Nematbakhsh, and B. S. Ghahfarokhi, "Context-aware multi-objective resource allocation in mobile cloud," Computers & Electrical Engi- neering, vol. 44, pp. 218 – 240, 2015.

S. Kikuchi and Y. Matsumoto, "What will happen if cloud management operations burst out?" in Integrated Network Management (IM), 2011 IFIP/IEEE International Symposium on, May 2011, pp. 97–104.

S. Shen, V. van Beek, and A. Iosup, "Statistical Characterization of Business-Critical Workloads Hosted in Cloud Datacenters," IEEE/ACM International Symposium on Cluster, Cloud and Grid Computing (CCGrid), 2015.

S. Yeganeh, A. Tootoonchian, and Y. Ganjali, "On scalability of software-defined networking," Communications Magazine, IEEE, vol. 51, no. 2, pp. 136–141, February 2013.

S. Zaman and D. Grosu, "Combinatorial auction-based allocation of virtual machine instances in clouds," in 2010 IEEE Second International Conference on Cloud Computing Technology and Science (CloudCom), Nov 2010, pp. 127–134.

S. Zhang, Z. Qian, J. Wu, and S. Lu, "SEA: Stable resource al- location in geographically distributed clouds," in Communications (ICC), 2014 IEEE International Conference on, June 2014, pp. 2932– 2937.

SAKURAI, Y., M. YOKoo, AND S. MATSUBARa: "A Limitation of the Generalized Vickrey Auction in Electronic Commerce: Robustness Against False-Name Bids," Proceedings of the Sixteenth National Conference on Artificial Intelligence, pp. 86–92, 1999.

Sher, Itai, Optimal Shill Bidding in the VCG Mechanism, Minnesota Research Report No. 2008-04, May 21, 2009.

t. S. Jain, "B47: Experience with a globally-deployed software defined wan," ACM SIGCOMM Computer Communication Review, vol. 43, 2013.

t. A.N. Quttoum, "A collusion-resistant mechanism for autonomic resource management in virtual private networks," Computer Communications, vol. 33, pp. 2070–2078, 2010.

T. Anderson, L. Peterson, S. Shenker, and J. Turner, "Overcoming the Internet Impasse Through Virtualization," Computer, vol. 38, no. 4, pp. 34–41, Apr. 2005.

T. Benson, A. Akella, A. Shaikh, and S. Sahu, "CloudNaaS: A Cloud Networking Platform for Enterprise Applications," in Proceedings of the 2Nd ACM Symposium on Cloud Computing, ser. SOCC '11. New York, NY, USA: ACM, 2011, pp. 8:1–8:13.

T. Genez, L. Bittencourt, and E. Madeira, "Workflow scheduling for SaaS / PaaS cloud providers considering two SLA levels," in Network Operations and Management Symposium (NOMS), 2012 IEEE, April 2012, pp. 906–912.

T. Wood, P. Shenoy, A. Venkataramani, and M. Yousif, "Black-box and Gray-box Strategies for Virtual Machine Migration," in Proceedings of the 4th USENIX Conference on Networked Systems Design & Implementation, ser. NSDI'07. Berkeley, CA, USA: USENIX Association, 2007, pp. 17–17.

The Vickrey-Clarke-Groves Mechanism work is licensed under the Creative Commons Attribution-NonCommercial-ShareAlike 3.0 License, Jeffrey Ely, July 8, 2009

U. Sharma, P. Shenoy, S. Sahu, and A. Shaikh, "Kingfisher: Cost-aware elasticity in the cloud," in INFOCOM, 2011 Proceedings IEEE, April 2011, pp. 206–210.

V. D. Blondel, J.-L. Guillaume, R. Lambiotte, and E. Lefebvre, “Fast unfolding of communities in large networks,” Journal of Statistical Mechanics: Theory and Experiment, vol. 2008, no. 10, p. P10008, 2008.

V. Emeakaroha, I. Brandic, M. Maurer, and I. Breskovic, “SLA-Aware Application Deployment and Resource Allocation in Clouds,” in Computer Software and Applications Conference Workshops (COMPSACW), 2011 IEEE 35th Annual, July 2011, pp. 298–303.

V. Issarny, N. Georgantas, S. Hachem, A. Zarras, P. Vassiliadis, M. Autili, M. A. Gerosa, and A. B. Hamida, “Service-Oriented Middleware for the Future Internet: State of the Art and Research Directions,” Journal of Internet Services and Appli- cations (JISA), pp. 1–23, Jun. 2011.

V. Mann, A. Vishnoi, K. Kannan, and S. Kalyanaraman, “CrossRoads: Seamless VM mobility across data centers through software defined networking,” in Network Operations and Management Symposium (NOMS), 2012 IEEE, April 2012, pp. 88– 96.

V. Shrivastava, P. Zerfos, K.-W. Lee, H. Jamjoom, Y.-H. Liu, and S. Banerjee, “Application-aware virtual machine migration in data centers,” in INFOCOM, 2011 Proceedings IEEE, April 2011, pp. 66–70.

V. Tsiatsis, A. Gluhak, T. Bauge, F. Montagut, J. Bernat, M. Bauer, C. Villalonga, P. Barnaghi, and S. Krco, The SENSEI Real World Internet Architecture, “Towards the Future Internet - Emerging Trends from European Research”. IOS Press, 2010, pp. 247–256.

Varian, Hal R., and Christopher Harris. 2014. "The VCG Auction in Theory and Practice." American Economic Review, 104 (5): 442-45. DOI: 10.1257/aer.104.5.442.

Vickrey-Clarke-Groves Mechanisms, Economics 285, Market Design, Jonathan Levin, Paul Milgrom's Winter 2009.

W. Grover, "How a network can think globally and act locally" and avoid the hazards of incoherence in distributed state information," in Transparent Optical Networks, 2007. CTON '07. 9th International Conference on, vol. 3, July 2007, pp. 178–182.

W. Dally and B. Towles, Principles and Practices of Interconnection Networks. San Francisco, CA, USA: Morgan Kaufmann Publishers Inc., 2003.

X. Meng, C. Isci, J. Kephart, L. Zhang, E. Bouillet, and D. Pendarakis, "Efficient Resource Provisioning in Compute Clouds via VM Multiplexing," in Proceedings of the 7th International Conference on Autonomic Computing, ser. ICAC '10. New York, NY, USA: ACM, 2010, pp. 11–20.

X. Meng, V. Pappas, and L. Zhang, "Improving the Scalability of Data Center Net- works with Traffic-aware Virtual Machine Placement," in INFOCOM, 2010 Proceed- ings IEEE, March 2010, pp. 1–9.

X. Wen, G. Gu, Q. Li, Y. Gao, and X. Zhang, "Comparison of open-source cloud management platforms: OpenStack and OpenNebula," in Fuzzy Systems and Knowledge Discovery (FSKD), 2012 9th International Conference on, May 2012, pp. 2457–2461.

X. Wen, K. Chen, Y. Chen, Y. Liu, Y. Xia, and C. Hu, "VirtualKnotter: Online Virtual Machine Shuffling for Congestion Resolving in Virtualized Datacenter," in Proceedings of the 2012 IEEE 32Nd International Conference on Distributed Com- puting Systems, ser. ICDCS '12. Washington, DC, USA: IEEE Computer Society, 2012, pp. 12–21.

X. Zhang, Z.-Y. Shae, S. Zheng, and H. Jamjoom, “Virtual machine migration in an over-committed cloud,” in Network Operations and Management Symposium (NOMS), 2012 IEEE, April 2012, pp. 196–203.

Z. Lu, J. Wu, and W. Fu, “A Novel Cloud-Oriented WS-Management-Based Resource Management Model,” in Web Services (ICWS), 2010 IEEE International Conference on, July 2010, pp. 676–677.

Z. Yusoh and M. Tang, “Composite SaaS placement and resource optimization in cloud computing using evolutionary algorithms,” in Cloud Computing (CLOUD), 2012 IEEE 5th International Conference on, June 2012, pp. 590–597.

Zeratul Izzah Mohd Yusoh, Maolin Tang, “A penalty-based grouping genetic algorithm for multiple composite SaaS com- ponents clustering in cloud,” in Systems, Man, and Cybernetics (SMC), 2012 IEEE International Conference on, Oct 2012, pp. 1396–1401.

[illegible] Z. W. Shao [illegible] [illegible] allocation of [illegible] in [illegible] computing [illegible] [illegible] [illegible] (NOMS), [illegible] [illegible] 2012 [illegible]

[illegible] [illegible] Fu [illegible] [illegible] [illegible] [illegible] [illegible] [illegible] [illegible] [illegible] [illegible] 2010, pp. [illegible]

[illegible] method [illegible] [illegible] [illegible] [illegible] [illegible] computing [illegible] Cloud Computing (CLOUD), 2012 IEEE 5th International Conference on, 2012, pp. 590-597.

[illegible] [illegible] based [illegible] [illegible] [illegible] [illegible] Systems, Man, and Cybernetics (SMC), 2012 IEEE International Conference on, 2012, pp. 1396-1401.

www.ingramcontent.com/pod-product-compliance
Lightning Source LLC
LaVergne TN
LVHW082338200926
848481LV00012B/3380